COOL DAWN

COOL DAWN

My National Velvet

Dido Harding

MAINSTREAM
PUBLISHING

EDINBURGH AND LONDON

First published in Great Britain in 1999 by
MAINSTREAM PUBLISHING COMPANY (EDINBURGH) LTD
7 Albany Street
Edinburgh EH1 3UG

ISBN 1 84018 179 6

A catalogue record for this book is available from the British Library

Flap photograph of the author courtesy of Georgina Taylor
Back photograph of the author and Cool Dawn courtesy of Linda Charles

Typeset in Sabon
Printed and bound in Great Britain by Butler & Tanner Ltd

To my husband, John – for always being there for me, no matter how insane my racing ambitions might be.

Contents

Acknowledgements

To Robert and Sally Alner without whom Cool Dawn's racing success would never have been possible. Locketts will always be my 'health club'.

To everyone involved at Locketts who have loved and cherished Dawn over the years every bit as much as I have, especially Andy who rides him, Jason who looks after him and Kathy who keeps the whole yard on the straight and narrow.

To the Cool Dawn fan club for being there to support us through thick and thin.

To my parents for never missing a race and pretending they don't find it terrifying when I ride.

To Andrew Thornton for riding Dawn so magnificently and making it as painless as possible for me to give up the ride.

To the members of the Portman Hunt for being so understanding of Dawn and me on the hunting field.

To the Costello and McCarthy families for selling me such a nice safe 'ladies' point-to-pointer'.

To Hils and Hugh for endless hours of book editing and to Georgie for being the official fan club photographer.

Chapter One

The Beginning

I grew up in the north of Dorset near Sherborne. My father had a small farm in a beautiful village called Nether Compton where he kept pigs and sheep and grew cider apples. I was a day girl at a local convent school, St Anthony's, Leweston, and spent most weekends and holidays riding around the farm and the surrounding country lanes on a succession of small, round ponies. We had a couple of stables and the horses were turned out in the cider-apple orchards for most of the year – except when the apples were getting too ripe and just too juicy for them to ignore. Dad kept a hunter throughout my childhood. He and I spent each winter hunting and most of the summers taking my ponies to a succession of local gymkhanas. Our enthusiasm was such that when Dave, my youngest brother, was born, Dad and I happily informed Mum that we wouldn't be home when she and the new baby returned from hospital because we had a horse show to attend. This has probably coloured both Mum's and Dave's attitude to horses ever since.

My first mounted competition was at the Chilcompton Show in 1972, when I was four. One of my schoolfriends had told me about the show and I was determined to take part. I was so overexcited I insisted that we get to the show in time for the first class at half past eight in the morning just in case my pony, Taffy, and I were eligible for it. Mum, Dad, my other brother Will, Taffy and I duly arrived to discover that the first class we could enter was at four in the afternoon. I didn't mind too much about that, in fact I had a wonderful time watching all the horses and ponies, but I suspect it might have been quite a long, boring day for my parents and my brother.

The class open to four year olds and their ten-hand two-inch ponies was the 'leading rein Monte Carlo'. This proved to be an exercise where all the children were led around the ring on their ponies by one of their parents to the sound of music. In each of the four corners of the ring there was a large playing card, one for each of the four card suits. The judge stood in the middle of the ring and cut a pack of cards. When the music stopped every contestant chose a corner and those in the corner that corresponded to the suit cut by the judge were eliminated. This carried on until there was only one contestant left. It had been a long day and I was bursting with excitement as Dad led Taffy and me into the ring. The music played and we circled around, then the music stopped and we hurried into the nearest corner expectantly. The judge duly cut the pack of cards and ten seconds later our corner was eliminated. That was that. My first gymkhana was over. I should have been disheartened, my parents certainly were, but I couldn't wait for more.

My first equine ambition was to be a three-day eventer. Lucinda Prior Palmer, as she was then, won the Badminton Horse Trials when I was seven and I was one of her biggest fans. She was only eighteen and she and her horse, Be Fair, had started off in the Pony Club just like me. As I trotted my pony along the narrow Dorset lanes I imagined we were on the roads and tracks phase of Badminton and that the cross-country course was just around the next corner.

The only problem with my already sky-high ambitions was that they weren't matched by my ability. I was about ten when I entered my first Pony Club one-day event. Unfortunately my pony, Polly, and I didn't get very far. I forgot part of the dressage test, then Polly refused the first fence of the show-jumping three times. From there it got worse as we stopped once at each of the first three fences on the cross-country, which meant that we were eliminated from all three phases of the competition without completing one of them.

At first my parents thought the problem might be the pony rather than the rider. Dad went off to view an alternative pony for me. He rode the pony and it quickly bucked him off. The pony's owner suggested that it was probably a bit too advanced for Dad and me. Dad took this criticism very badly and immediately bought the pony to prove her wrong. Unfortunately, the vendor couldn't have been more right and within months the pony was on the market again.

When I was fourteen, Mum and Dad bought me my first real horse hoping that this would start me on the road to Badminton. The horse was not everyone's idea of a sensible schoolmaster. She was a six-year-old, three-quarter thorough-bred chestnut mare called Rosie. Rosie was very headstrong and stubborn, and I have to confess that we were probably too alike to get on very well. In our first dressage contest Rosie did not like staying within the white boards that surrounded the ring and tried to jump them to escape. When I kicked her in the ribs to keep her straight she simply bucked me off. Another elimination and we seemed to be back where we started. It didn't look as if I would ever reach Badminton.

While I was clearly no good at dressage, I had always loved speed. Aged six I could be found watching the Saturday racing on TV from the back of my rocking-horse, riding out the finish for all I was worth. And Rosie did know how to gallop. She and I raced Dad on his hunter around the farm at top speed pretending all the time that we were fighting out the finish of the Grand National. I took Rosie hunting and, although she rarely agreed to jump anything, she and I proved just how fast we could go by regularly overtaking the Field Master at a flat-out gallop.

A year later, when Rosie and I still weren't getting on well together, Dad suggested that we sell her and buy a horse that was better suited to my temperament. I had faced up to the fact that I didn't have the skill to compete at Badminton and wanted a nice horse to take hunting and maybe compete in the occasional hunter trial or team chase.

We found a five-year-old part thoroughbred called Minsara who looked as if he fitted the bill nicely. His owner, Jack Wetherall, let us have him on a week's trial over half term and he seemed to be just what the doctor ordered. He was much calmer than Rosie and jumped well out hunting without going crazy. There was just one condition: Mrs Wetherall was very worried that we might be tempted to race Minsara and she made Dad and I promise that we weren't planning to point-to-point him. Dad had ridden as an amateur in point-to-points and hunter chases when he was younger but, apart from my make-believe racing on the farm, it hadn't occurred to either of us that I would follow suit. So we promised faithfully and handed over two thousand pounds for Minsara.

For two seasons Minsara (or Sammy as we called him at home) and I had a great time hunting with the South Dorset Hunt. Their field master, Major Michael Dangerfield, was the father of one of my school friends, Georgina, and we spent many happy Saturdays careering round the Dorset country-side together. When Georgina and I weren't galloping flat out and jumping hedges, gates or any other obstacles we came across, we were trying to persuade the older members of the hunt to let us have a sip of whisky from their hip-flasks. We always thought that Michael didn't know what we were up to, but looking back I am almost certain he did.

Sammy seemed pretty fast and looked like a racehorse so it wasn't long before Mrs Wetherall's promise started niggling at my mind. Would he make a point-to-pointer, I wondered? As the hunting season came to an end in March, I went to watch the local point-to-point and came home convinced that Sammy and I would be up to the challenge. I didn't know much about point-to-pointing but it didn't look too different from jumping fences out hunting; it just had the added element of competition. Little did I know.

Dad had raced years before and tried to convince me that it wasn't quite that simple. He talked to the farmer who owned the local course and he let Sammy and me jump over a couple of the point-to-point fences the weekend after the races, in the hope that I would realise quite how difficult racing was. Sammy and I jumped two or three fences on our own at a fast canter and that was all it took – I was hooked. I had no idea how much more difficult it would be with twenty horses all around us, going at twice the speed Sammy and I could manage on our own. All I could think of was the thrill of winning a race. You could say it was a case of blind ambition and ignorance triumphing over common sense.

I was determined to get Sammy and me to the races the following year, no matter what we had promised Mrs Wetherall or how difficult it might be to get Sammy fit. I was due to go off to Oxford University that autumn, and after persistent badgering through the summer, Dad agreed that he would get Sammy fit and together we would try to point-to-point him the following spring.

That first season none of us knew very much about point-to-pointing. Dad had ridden once or twice as an amateur about twenty years earlier, as had my grandfather before the war, but things had changed a bit since then.

Point-to-points acquired their name when they were races across open country from one point to another. Nowadays they are amateur steeplechase meetings run along very much the same lines as a professional jump-racing event at the well-known racecourses like Cheltenham or Ascot.

Each hunt holds its own point-to-point for fun and for fund-raising with six or seven races in a day, and the season runs from January through to the end of May with racing at the weekends and on bank holidays. Usually all races are run over a standard course of about three miles and will include some twenty regulation steeplechase fences. The only major differences with professional steeplechasing are that point-to-point meetings are held on temporary racecourses that tend to revert to farmland for all but the day of the race, the fences are slightly smaller and easier to jump and all the horses, jockeys and trainers must be amateurs. The only qualification horse and jockey need is to have hunted regularly with their local pack of hounds. This left the way clear for ambitious nutters like me to have a go.

For point-to-pointing you don't need to register your riding colours with any official body, so you can wear pretty much anything you like. Mum volunteered to knit my colours and together we designed something that we thought would be easy for spectators – well, Mum – to spot. My favourite colour was blue, so we came up with a blue and white design with a blue body, white sleeves and a white zig-zag down the middle like a bolt of lightning. There was little chance of anyone having the same colours as Sammy and me.

The sport may be amateur in name but it is extremely competitive and has become a very serious business. Getting a horse fit for a three-mile race is an accomplishment in itself. In any one year there are some four thousand horses competing in point-to-points, and many of them are every bit as fit as their professional counterparts. It had been a very long time since Dad had prepared a horse to race, I had never done anything like it and, of course, Sammy had never seen a racecourse in his life. Sammy was incredibly lazy and we did not find it easy to get him fit on his own at home.

By the start of the season we thought Sammy was ready for his first race. I suspect any experienced trainer would have taken one look at his large belly swinging from side to side as he walked round the paddock and said he that he was at least two months away from being racing fit. But how were we to know?

Dad was insistent that two novices should not be allowed to have their first race together so he arranged for a local amateur, Steven Stickland, to ride Sammy in his first race at Badbury Rings. I got up at six in the morning to plait Sammy's mane and tail and Dad and I felt very proud of ourselves when we drove in through the 'horseboxes only' entrance. Steven kindly guided Dad and me through the routine of weighing out and saddling and it wasn't long before Sammy was having the first race of his life. He was completely exhausted after the first mile and a half when Steven pulled him up, but at least he jumped pretty well, so Dad agreed that I could ride him in his second race.

My first race will not go down in history as a great success. We did win the best turned-out prize (ten pounds given to the groom of the horse judged to be the best presented when the horses walked round the paddock) but that was probably because all my tack was brand new and the judge was the Wetherall's daughter. Despite the fact that we had broken our promise not to race Sammy, the Wetherall family seemed pleased that we were getting so much pleasure from him and that he was obviously well loved.

I wasn't nervous at the start because I didn't really know what to expect, and I certainly wasn't ready for the horses to go as fast as they did. I couldn't believe we were actually jumping fences at that speed. I equally wasn't prepared for riding in a racing saddle with short stirrups. Over the first fence I lost a stirrup and only just got it back by the time the second fence arrived, when I did the same again. I bounced and bumped around in the saddle, and it's a miracle that Sammy was able to keep himself balanced enough not to fall over on the flat, let alone jump the fences. He jumped well for the first half of the race and then started to get very tired; he wasn't the only one. I wasn't anywhere near fit enough to race-ride and was puffing very hard as well. Sammy and I may not have known anything about point-to-pointing but we did know a little bit about avoiding disaster, so we pulled up with half a circuit left to go.

Race-riding is a strangely addictive sport. The first time

you ride at over thirty miles an hour over four-and-a-half-foot-high obstacles with horses behind and in front, you are either instantly hooked or you never want to do something so insane ever again. I was completely addicted. We may have pulled up with no chance of winning but it was the most thrilling and exhilarating thing I had ever done. I couldn't wait for the next race and dreamt of being 'in the money' for the first time.

I returned to Oxford completely pumped up and ready for our next race but determined to get fit. In addition to adopting most traditional training methods – running or going to the gym – I read a book that suggested riding a bicycle with no seat. Throughout that spring I could be seen frantically pedalling up the High on a bike with very small wheels, obviously in too low a gear and with no saddle – not a traditional form of transport, even in Oxford.

It took several more races before Sammy and I completed our first point-to-point. We were last in the Ladies' Race at the Blackmore and Sparkford Vale point-to-point at Kingweston, finishing more than a fence behind the winner – but we did finish. You would have thought we had just won the Grand National the amount of celebrating that went on when Sammy and I appeared triumphantly back at the horsebox. But even in those early days I learnt that racing has its ups and its downs. A few weeks later we ran at Badbury Rings in Dorset. Sammy hit the fourth-last fence very hard and catapulted me out of the saddle and head first into the ground. I had fallen off countless ponies in my childhood but nothing had prepared me for quite how painful it was to hit the ground at a flat-out gallop and then be trampled on by the following horses. I lay on the ground for a few minutes out of breath and very sore while Mum and Dad tried to do a four-minute mile across the course to get to me. In fact I was just winded, as were they by the time they reached me, but it was a rude awakening to the realities of a very dangerous sport.

Dad had found it very hard to get Sammy fit on his own,

so a family friend who had seen us finishing at Kingweston, Biddy Wingfield-Digby, kindly offered to take over Sammy's training after his first season. Biddy had been Master of the Blackmore and Sparkford Vale Hunt, and her son Jack rode in point-to-points, so she had several racehorses in a small yard at Hazelbury Bryan in Dorset. Biddy did an enormous amount to improve my riding, and she helped Sammy and me achieve our first placing – second in a maiden the following year, again at Kingweston. It had taken us two seasons just to be placed for the first time, but I was starting to feel like I was really getting the hang of things.

A year later, still with Biddy, Sammy won for the first time, but sadly I was not in the saddle. I was away skiing and Nick Mitchell, the son of a local professional trainer, partnered Sammy instead. I called from Italy to hear the great news that Sammy had finally won a race, but I couldn't help but feel a little sad that I hadn't been riding. It wasn't until the next year that I had my first win and Sammy had his second; together we won a restricted race at Larkhill. It had taken us more than twenty races together to win, but win we eventually did.

After three years with Biddy, Sammy moved to the nearby point-to-pointing yard run by Robert Alner because Biddy's husband was ill and she didn't have the time to devote to her horses. Robert was one of the top point-to-point jockeys in the country and had at least twenty horses at Locketts, his dairy farm. It all felt a lot more sophisticated and we were very honoured to be included.

Sammy and I had our second win together – a ladies' open at Badbury Rings, which we won by over twenty lengths. We still would not have counted ourselves among the most stylish or successful partnerships in the West Country but we were having fun. At Easter I went skiing with my family and agreed to let Robert run Sammy while we were away. But, unfortunately, Sammy ran badly and the following day was very lame. I called from the French Alps to find out how the race had gone, and discovered that my horse was unlikely to be able to race ever again. He had badly damaged a flexor tendon and, at the very least, would be out of action for a year.

I was very sad that my precious horse was hurt, but things have a funny way of working out. That spring I had applied to study for a Masters in Business Administration (MBA) at Harvard Business School and I was due to spend the following two years in the United States. So even if Sammy had been racing fit, I wouldn't have been able to ride him. Sammy had run over thirty races and given me two fantastic wins, which was more than I probably deserved, and he, at twelve years old, was at the tail end of his racing career. That autumn I set off to Harvard to study and Sammy was retired to grass, and both of us forgot about racing for a while . . .

I can honestly say that for two years I really didn't think about horses and racing very much at all. The MBA course at Harvard is one of the toughest in the world and for much of the time I was simply working too hard. When I wasn't working there were new friends to make from around the globe, skiing in Vermont and the whole of the rest of the US to explore. I don't think many of my friends from Harvard even knew that I liked horses.

After my two-year course I went to London to work for McKinsey, a management consultancy firm, but it wasn't long before horses came back into my life. I returned to England in October, when the nights are starting to get longer and the cold winter weather draws in. Good hunting weather in other words. With no skiing within easy reach and weekends no longer filled with college parties, I thought it was about time I started riding again.

One Friday, I went down to Dorset to stay with my parents for the weekend and on the off chance called Robert Alner to see if he needed an extra jockey on the gallops the following morning. There aren't many trainers, amateur or professional, who will turn away an extra free pair of hands, even with my race-riding track record, and the next morning I was being legged up on to one of Robert's horses.

The yard had changed a lot in two years, not least because Harry Wellstead was now in charge of the point-to-pointers. Robert still rode them in races, but he had started training with a Jockey Club permit. Although this was not the same as being a fully professional trainer it did mean that Robert could train horses to run in full-blown National Hunt races. Everything seemed bigger and more professional than I remembered. The previous season Robert had won the point-to-point jockey's championship and had ridden his two hundredth winner – considering I had all of two winners to my name it was a fairly humbling thought.

That first day I rode a wonderful, experienced ex-point-to-pointer called Ocean Link. He had won five times the previous season with Robert in the saddle. Great things were expected of him this year in professional races. It was fantastic to be on the back of a racehorse again and I found it hard to believe that I had gone two years without horses. By the time I got back to London at the end of the weekend I had decided I wanted to get back into racing. It was just a question of how.

Sammy had enjoyed his two-year break and his leg was looking better, but at fourteen it wasn't realistic to expect him to restart his racing career. If I was going to race-ride again I needed another mount. With my record no one was likely to let me ride their horse, so I was going to have to buy something myself. The only problem with this plan was money. Harvard is not a cheap place to study for two years. Although McKinsey had paid most of the fees, I had still run up an enormous overdraft. The bank had let me run up the debts on the assumption that once I was back in England I would be in a well-paid consulting job and would repay their loan within a year or two. I am sure they weren't expecting me to buy a horse as well.

What's more I didn't want to buy just any old horse. I wanted to be as sure as I could be that the horse was going to be good. I didn't really want to spend the next two years waiting for the first time the horse would be placed in a maiden, as we had with Sammy. Instead, I hoped to buy something that would be capable of winning ladies' opens with me on a regular basis and, with luck, go on to run in a hunter chase or two. I asked Harry and Robert how much it would cost to buy a horse like that, which also jumped well enough for me to be safe. They felt seven thousand pounds would be enough to buy a promising young horse who would win ladies' opens with me. This was a good deal more than I had to spare, it was over three times more than we'd paid for Minsara and was not a sum that I would be able to hide from the bank manager. I was going to have to ask for an extension to my business school loans.

The next week I gathered all my courage together and phoned my bank manager, Ron Barnes at Barclays Bank in London, who has looked after McKinsey employees going to business school for many years. He was completely accustomed to receiving loan-extension requests to buy BMWs and expensive holidays but I think my horse was a first. To my surprise he didn't seem too fazed and agreed to let me buy a horse provided I didn't go over my budget of seven thousand pounds. I was in business.

For the next six months Robert scoured the sales catalogues for me. I asked him to help because I knew I was such a softy that I would buy the first horse I found that looked in need of a home. Robert was always on the look-out for good horses at all the major sales so he would cast a much more discerning eye than me. Together we went to Doncaster sales in the spring and looked at several hundred horses. I found several I liked, but Robert would only let me consider one or two. All of them went above my seven-thousand-pound limit in the sale ring. By May we still hadn't found a horse that Robert considered suitable and that I could afford.

At the end of the point-to-point season Robert went to Ireland on a shopping trip. He was looking for horses for a number of people, including potential owners for his own new professional yard. He would keep an eye out for anything that might suit me. As we had seen hundreds of horses together and I knew he was far fussier than I was, I gave him authority to buy without talking to me – provided he didn't exceed the seven-thousand-pound limit. I was working quite hard and didn't really think any more about it.

A week later I was checking my answerphone messages at the end of the day when I got to a message from Robert: 'Just calling to let you know that I've bought you a horse. He's exactly seven thousand pounds, and once he's passed the vet he should be with you in about a week. He's got quite a fun name – Cool Dawn. Can you send a cheque?' And that was that. I didn't know anything else about the horse and there was no going back. I had given Robert authority to buy and this unknown horse was mine.

A week later Dad and I went over to Locketts Farm to pick up my purchase and more of the story unfolded. Robert had been in the west of Ireland with a potential owner, Anne Young, who was looking for a mare to race and then breed from. Anne is the sister of top Irish trainer Harry de Bromhead and shares a house in Dorset with her barrister husband David. Robert had seen Cool Dawn and liked him, but the price his owner, Mr McCarthy, wanted was above my limit. Robert, Anne and Mr McCarthy had adjourned to a local pub, bought a bottle of whiskey and continued discussing horses. Every so often Robert and Mr McCarthy had disappeared outside to continue negotiations over Cool Dawn and Anne filled up everyone's whiskey glass. It is probably a miracle that they could all remember which horse was being bought, but eventually the whiskey bottle was drained and the deal was done

Cool Dawn was a five-year-old bay gelding standing a good sixteen hands three inches tall. He had raced in several point-to-points in Ireland, but the best place he had managed was third. On all occasions he had jumped extremely well, but he didn't seem to stay. He looked very weak and thin, and Robert hoped that if he strengthened up he should stay three miles with only eleven stone on his back in ladies' opens. What we did not know at the time was that his Irish point-to-point form really wasn't as bad as it seemed. In two of his races he was beaten by horses that went on to be some of the top chasers of their generation: Gales Cavelier and Unguided Missile. At that time they were just young Irish point-to-pointers being sold as potential novice chasers, but they had made Cool Dawn look distinctly average.

My new purchase seemed kind and friendly and Dad and I took him home with the promise to Robert that we would feed him several pounds of nuts every day. He was turned out in my parents' paddock with Sammy and they couldn't have been more different. Sammy had put on an enormous amount of weight since retiring while Cool Dawn was all skin and bone. Every day Dad tried his best to fill Cool Dawn full of nuts while preventing Sammy getting any fatter but, as hard as he tried, I fear the older horse often got the better of the feeding arrangements.

We were meant to leave Cool Dawn alone in his field to acclimatise after his journey from Ireland and on no account was I meant to ride him. But after a month watching him relax in the field I couldn't bear it any longer. I had to see what a seven-thousand-pound horse was like to sit on.

I tied Sammy up to the gate to watch while I tacked up Cool Dawn in the field. Mum, Dad and my boyfriend, John Penrose, looked on while I heaved myself up into the saddle and trotted my new purchase around the field. He felt absolutely enormous and I was dying to see what his canter was like. When I kicked him on he arched his back and put in a large buck. Much excitement amongst the spectators, but at least I could tell that he had a huge stride. He didn't have any shoes on, otherwise I would have taken him on a gentle ride along the roads, so we had to call it a day after another circuit of the field. I didn't know what an expensive racehorse was meant to feel like, but he seemed good to me.

At the end of August my whole family was due to spend a week on holiday in Scotland and Mum and Dad were very nervous about leaving my expensive new horse and Sammy unattended in their field. Cool Dawn wasn't due to join Harry Wellstead for another six weeks and Sammy's pony companion, Badger, was away with friends for the summer holidays, so even if Harry took Cool Dawn early we still needed to do something with Sammy. A neighbour kindly volunteered to feed them both and check them over every day but in the end that wasn't necessary.

The evening before we were all due to drive to Scotland Cool Dawn became horribly lame. We needed to leave first thing the next day and we didn't have time to wait for the vet to arrive, let alone make arrangements for whatever treatment was necessary. In desperation I called Locketts and asked if they would have room for Cool Dawn earlier than expected, complete with Sammy until his pony companion returned. There was a stunned silence when I explained that Cool Dawn was lame and Robert instantly reassured me that I could bring them both over early the following day.

Dad had an old horse trailer that he towed behind his Ford Sierra. It was a bit small to fit two racehorses in and didn't have a partition. Fortunately Sammy and Cool Dawn were firm friends and didn't seem to mind. At six o'clock in the morning I set off for Locketts with the two of them in the trailer behind me. My parents lived about a forty-minute drive away and I was keen to get back so we could leave for Scotland at eight o'clock. About half-way into the journey I stopped at a T-junction in Sherborne and turned sharp right. As the trailer rounded the corner I heard a loud bang which prompted me to look in the wing mirror. I could see straw and a bit of loose wood on the ground about a foot behind the trailer. I knew that there shouldn't be anything on the road and I suddenly realised the old wooden floor of the trailer had collapsed. In a panic, I pulled the car and trailer over on to the first bit of flat ground I found and very nervously opened the side door to see what was going on inside. I couldn't believe what I saw. Cool Dawn was standing calmly on his side of the trailer, but on the other side Sammy was standing on three legs with a huge hole in the floor under his near hind leg. The floor had rotted and broken away under Sammy's great weight. It was half past six in the morning and there was no one to be seen anywhere. I was going to have to leave the horses to try and telephone for help. I ran a hundred yards down the road to a phone box I could see in the distance and in a complete panic called Robert and explained what had happened.

A lame Cool Dawn had been bad enough the day before, but I really rendered Robert speechless this time. He was about to set out for racing and didn't have a spare lorry that could come and rescue us, but he arranged for a local haulier, Paddy Foot, to come out immediately to help. I went back to the trailer and spent a very nervous half an hour trying to keep calm so as not to upset the horses.

Thank goodness the floor had given way under Sammy and not Cool Dawn. At least he was old enough and wise enough not to panic. My young horse might not have been so calm. Finally Paddy arrived and we reversed Cool Dawn out of the box quite easily though he was clearly lame. It was much harder for Sammy to get out and avoid the hole and he nearly fell through it completely. By the time he came down the ramp he had a nasty cut on his near hind and looked quite lame as well. Paddy went on to Locketts to deliver my two injured horses while I turned around and headed back home to go on to Scotland. It was not the best start to Cool Dawn's career in England, but certainly a memorable one.

Fortunately, by the time the Harding family returned from Scotland, both horses were almost recovered. Cool Dawn had thin soles to his hooves, so his feet had got very sore on the hard ground at home but a set of shoes had sorted him out quite quickly. Sammy's near hind was healing well, and he had thoroughly enjoyed being back at his old racing home.

Harry suggested that Cool Dawn should stay at Locketts as it was so close to the start of the hunting season, but I think the truth was that he was worried about what would happen if Cool Dawn returned to the Harding family. Sammy went home to my parents once the school holidays ended and his companion, Badger, was back in the field too. I settled down to wait for Cool Dawn's first point-to-point season, all the time hoping that we might win one race if we were lucky.

Chapter Two

The First Season

To qualify horses for point-to-pointing they have to go hunting at least seven times between October and January each year. So before we could begin to put my racing dreams into action, Cool Dawn and I had to hunt.

Dawn, as the stable had imaginatively nicknamed him, started gentle exercise in early October. By the beginning of November he was fit enough to stand an easy day's hunting, but not so fit that he would be too dangerous. Well, that was the theory.

Our first day's hunting with the Portman Hunt was at Guy's Marsh, near Shaftesbury, on a typically grey, damp Saturday in November. Dad had sold our old trailer once it had been repaired, so I didn't have any transport of my own. Harry arranged for the Alners to lend me their lorry, but didn't realise that it was the first time I had ever driven a proper horse lorry. My best friend, Hils, was staying with my parents for the weekend and she kindly agreed to keep me company in the lorry while Mum and Dad drove directly to the meet. I was terrified of using the brakes too sharply and knocking Dawn over inside so I drove as slowly as I possibly could. I thought the speedometer was in miles per hour and that we were travelling at a respectable thirty miles an hour. It was only when Hils looked behind and saw an enormous queue of cars (and furious drivers) behind me that we realised we were actually dawdling through the narrow country lanes at twenty-five kilometres an hour, (fifteen miles an hour). Even then it felt pretty fast and I think the sight of a large lorry driven by two small, scared blonde girls was enough to frighten the oncoming traffic to a standstill. Both of us were extremely relieved when we arrived in one piece.

At the meet, I had quite a struggle to persuade Dawn to stand still and not to kick the living daylights out of the hounds, foot followers or small ponies who were all crammed on to the small village green. The hounds found a fox as soon as we left the meet, and the mounted followers set off at a gallop along a narrow lane. I was concentrating so hard on keeping Dawn from barging into the horse in front of us that I didn't see the jump at the end of the lane until it was too late. As we thundered towards what was a pretty substantial five-bar gate, Rosie Babbington, a keen member of the Portman Hunt and who was riding a safe and sensible hunter, yelled out: 'Have you ever jumped anything on that horse? Would you like a lead?' But there was no way Dawn would let any horse get past him to give him a lead – he knew he was a racehorse and being overtaken was strictly against the rules. So we careered towards the gate at top speed and to everyone's surprise, except Dawn's, sailed over in style.

The Portman had a fine day's hunting that Saturday and I soon discovered that there was, quite literally, nothing that Dawn wouldn't jump. Midway through the afternoon we were queuing to jump a post and rails in the corner of a field, when an old hunter in front of us refused. Dawn didn't see the problem and tried to jump horse, rider and fence all at once. He succeeded, but unfortunately the old hunter, its rider and I didn't and we were all left sprawling on the ground as Dawn galloped away. There was never any doubt from then on that he loved jumping.

At the end of the day, after narrowly surviving another hair-raising drive in the lorry, I returned Dawn to his stable at Locketts and I joined Robert and his wife Sally for tea. They had seen Dawn gallop with the other point-to-pointers the week before and had not been particularly impressed with his performance. When I related our adventures to them over a cup of tea in their kitchen, they tried hard to reassure me that even if he proved no good on the racecourse, he would always make a fantastic team chaser.

By the end of January, Dawn and I had survived our seven days' hunting, the Portman Hunt breathed a collective sigh of relief and it was time to focus on racing. Before our first planned race, it seemed sensible to jump a couple of practice steeplechase fences. Robert was schooling a number of Harry Wellstead's point-to-pointers on a Sunday morning, and he suggested that Dawn and I join him. Also in the schooling party was another amateur jockey: Suzannah Barraclough. Suzannah had ridden successfully in point-to-points and hunter chases and had just bought an experienced chaser called Joyful Noise to ride against professionals in handicaps. Joyful Noise had jumped round the Grand National fences and was far more experienced than any of the young point-to-pointers Robert would be schooling. He and Suzannah seemed ideal schooling partners for Dawn and me.

Robert suggested that Suzannah and I jumped side by side over three steeplechase fences that were lined up against the hedge in one of his fields. The intention was that we would trot the two horses to the bottom of the field, turn them to face the line of three fences, then jump all three together at a reasonable gallop. I was more than a little nervous about this plan. As well as Robert, there were five or six lads from the yard watching on horses waiting to be schooled. I could have done without an audience for my first encounter with steeplechase fences in over three years. Dawn could sense my worries, and was really overexcited as Suzannah and I trotted our horses down to the bottom of the field as instructed. As soon as we turned round to face the fences Dawn grabbed the bit and leapt forward. Joyful Noise was keen too, and before

I had time to think we were hurtling towards the first fence at full speed. The two horses jumped the fence side by side, and as soon as Dawn landed he tugged hard at the reins and accelerated again, leaving our schooling partners a full length behind. We jumped the second fence even faster than the first and went another length ahead of Suzannah and Joyful Noise. Sammy had been a safe jumper but he certainly had never jumped at the speed that Dawn seemed to enjoy and by the time we had cleared the third fence I thought we would end up in orbit. Dawn seemed to gain rather than lose momentum in the air. I had never experienced anything like it.

Somehow I managed to persuade Dawn to stop and we rejoined Robert and the other lads for a debriefing. 'I'd try and go a little slower if you can, next time,' was all Robert said to me, and he sent us both off to do it again. Second time round Dawn knew exactly what to expect and he whipped around at the bottom of the field like a spinning top. We were already ahead of Joyful Noise by the time we reached the first and rather than worrying about the fences I was totally focused on how on earth I was going to apply the brakes before Dawn careered straight into the ditch at the end of the field.

'I meant slower, not faster,' was all Robert said this time, but he had a broad grin on his face, and I heard one of the lads say that it looked as if Dawn was giving Joyful Noise a jumping lesson, not the other way round. If Dawn could reproduce the same speed and enthusiasm on the racecourse, he looked like he might be a reasonable point-to-pointer after all. It would not be long before we found out, as our first race was planned for the following week.

Dawn's first outing was at the Hursley Hambledon point-to-point at Badbury Rings in Dorset. Badbury Rings, like virtually every other point-to-point course I've ever been to, is on the top of an exposed hill, with beautiful views and chilling winds no matter what time of year. Despite the cold weather, a select group of friends and family had come to support us. Mum and Dad had driven over from their new house in

Somerset with my brothers Will and Dave. John, my boy-friend, came from London for his first point-to-point ever with Hils, who, having witnessed our first day's hunting, was not going to miss our first race. Georgina Dangerfield and her father Michael, from my old South Dorset hunting days, were also in attendance. The Dangerfields had owned several good racehorses including All A Myth, a really successful point-to-pointer in the early 1970s. They thought I was completely mad to have bought any horse without even seeing it in advance, let alone one which cost as much as seven thousand pounds.

Things didn't get off to a good start when Hils and I tried to order drinks in the beer tent. All dressed up in my racing kit complete with my back protector I looked like an over-sized Barbie Doll in riding kit. No doubt my face was starting to go grey with fear as the barman took one look at me, refused to believe that I was over eighteen and wouldn't serve me. No amount of pleading would change his mind. In other circumstances, being considered seven years younger than I really was would have been a big morale boost, but at the time I badly needed a dose of Dutch courage, not to mention something to protect me from the freezing temperatures.

My confidence was improved by two of Harry's horses winning their races with consummate ease. Mr Murdock and Roving Report were both ridden by Robert, having his first race rides since breaking his leg in a nasty fall a year earlier. Robert made it all look so easy that he almost had me believing I could do it too.

By mid-afternoon the winter weather was starting to get the better of my friends and family. They were all blue with cold and muttering quietly about their preference for summer sports. Unbeknownst to me the lads from Locketts had told them all about our schooling session and, as a result, they had each put a fiver on us to win. It was a large, cold, but expectant group that greeted me as I walked into the paddock with the other jockeys.

Their money looked none too safe when Dawn reared up

just seconds after I had sat in the saddle. He went right over backwards leaving me with nowhere to go but down. I was flung into the air and landed on my back under the paddock railings with a thump, right at the feet of some bemused spectators. I had been nervous before, now I was in complete shock. I looked up at Harry Wellstead and Robert, hoping they would say that Dawn had cut himself and we would have to withdraw. But there was no escape, I was swiftly legged back into the saddle and told to get on with it.

As we cantered away I began to get really scared. Dawn was pulling hard and I was convinced that we would jump the first fence on our way down to the start – surely the most humiliating thing an amateur jockey could do. Somehow I managed to persuade him to stop in time and as we circled round the starter with the other fifteen runners, I asked myself what on earth I was doing riding such an inexperienced and headstrong horse. I knew I wasn't that good a horsewoman; even good jockeys have bad falls on young horses, so surely I was bound to have a nasty accident. I promised myself that I would never, ever, do this again. Next time I'd get an experienced jockey to ride Dawn for me – if I survived this time of course.

I was far too nervous to take in the rest of the runners at the time but the racecard says that there were sixteen in our race, the third division of the Open Maiden. The favourite was a horse called Quick Rapor, ridden by Dominic Alers-Hankey. They had been second the previous week and were trained by one of the top point-to-point trainers, Richard Barber. Next in the betting was General Moss, ridden by Mike Felton. Mike had been national champion point-to-point jockey in the past and was one of the most experienced amateur jockeys in the West Country. General Moss had never run, but word had obviously gone out that he was a potential winner. Next in the betting came Cool Dawn and me at 5–1. Dawn's short price was probably thanks to my family, friends and the lads who had seen us school, but I'm glad I didn't know that at the time, because it would have only added to my worries. The vast majority of the other horses had never seen a racecourse before, but I didn't even know that much about them – I was far too concerned about my own fate to worry about the opposition.

The starter called us up to the line, dropped the flag and we were off. I tried to block out my fear and remember my instructions, 'Don't interfere, let him see each fence and enjoy himself.' I can't really claim any responsibility for the fact that we followed those instructions. Dawn had no intention of letting me interfere. He took hold of the bit as we accelerated towards the first fence and that was that.

We were in second place for the first four fences, then jumped into the lead, which is where we stayed. Behind us Quick Rapor fell at the first and two other horses unseated their riders before the end of the first circuit. We came past the crowd in the lead the first time around with the rest of the field strung out behind us and I even dared to dream of what it would be like to be in the lead at the end of the next and final circuit. Dawn jumped each fence with the same enthusiasm that he had when schooling at home and I had never felt so safe in a race. He had taken a strong hold, but seemed to be going well within himself, totally in command of the situation. With four fences left to go we were still in the lead and I kept expecting horses to come charging past us, but all I could hear was the jockey behind me growling at his horse to go faster. The jockey in question was Mike Felton and the two of us were drawing further and further ahead of the rest of the field. I hadn't asked Dawn to quicken at all but over each fence we went a length ahead of General Moss. Mike Felton then urged his horse on to catch up with us between fences and each time Dawn jumped ahead again.

All of a sudden we were coming around the final bend towards the last fence and I couldn't believe we were still in the lead. Mike Felton was really putting General Moss under pressure, but they weren't gaining on us at all. All we had to do was jump the last. I heard Georgina yelling 'Come on, Dido' and it just didn't seem real. Dawn jumped the last as easily as he had all the others. I finally stopped holding on to his head and he duly accelerated away to win easily with six lengths between us and General Moss.

I know the jockey is meant to transmit confidence to the horse, but with us it seemed to be the other way round. Dawn was so confident of his own ability, that once the race had started all my pre-race nerves had evaporated and when we crossed the finishing line I wanted to do it all over again. It was incredible that we had won our first race and I couldn't wait for another dose of racing adrenaline. By the time I rode back into the winners' enclosure with a large grin on my face, there was no way I would have considered giving up the ride on him – ever.

My friends were on cloud nine. Dawn's victory was so unexpected and they'd made money out of it. We all wandered around Badbury Rings in a state of euphoria. No one noticed the freezing temperatures any more, especially when we heard that rumours were circulating that I'd paid thirty-five thousand pounds for Dawn. Even the Dangerfields had to admit that my expensive 'Irish Donkey' looked quite talented.

I had dreamt of winning a race on him one day, but never in my wildest dreams had I expected it to be first time out. As I left Badbury Rings for the long drive back to London, my final thought was that even though Dawn had had only one race, it really wouldn't matter if he never won again. He'd given everyone, and me especially so much pleasure that afternoon, he really didn't owe us anything more.

Dawn's second race was two weeks later at the South Dorset point-to-point. It was amazing how my expectations had changed in that time. Somehow, in the space of two weeks, I had managed to forget that Dawn's victory at Badbury Rings was unexpected and all of a sudden I did mind if he didn't win another race. In fact, now, only winning would do. I wasn't alone. My growing band of followers consisting of parents, brothers and friends, was quite happy to endure another cold, windswept hill, but they too expected victory. Mum and Dad, John, Hils and the Dangerfields were once again in attendance and I have a feeling that some of their winnings from the previous race were reinvested in expectation of another victory. The pressure was on.

Our race was the first of the day. Thanks to our victory at Badbury Rings we were no longer eligible for the maiden race (reserved for horses who have not won) and were now running in the restricted (reserved for horses who have won no more than one maiden and one restricted). The majority of our nine rivals had also won races and it was by no means certain that we would win again. Even so, the bookies started us off at 10–11 favourite. The other fancied horses were Earl Boon, ridden by Polly Curling, the reigning champion point-to-point jockey, and Fellow Countryman, ridden by his owner Andrew Wardle. Earl Boon had won his first race of the season but had been pulled up in his second, two weeks before the South Dorset. Fellow Countryman had not run yet that season but had won a maiden in impressive style the previous year. Buoyed up with our success at Badbury Rings we weren't afraid of them.

The South Dorset course at Milbourne St Andrew is a tight left-handed oval. There is a sharp left-hand corner into the finishing straight which you have to negotiate three times. In fact, the majority of the course is on the turn. It all seemed fairly straightforward when I walked the course and although my nerves set in again once I started to get changed into my racing kit, I could remember the excitement of winning so it was less scary. This time I was much more focused on winning.

Nick Freak, the stable blacksmith, and John Dufosee, another local point-to-point trainer, met me in the paddock together with the expectant fan club. Harry was one of the officials at the South Dorset point-to-point, and Robert was riding at another meeting, so Nick and John were there to look after us and prevent another rearing accident. Andy Miller, whose family farmed next to the Alners, led Dawn around. Andy often rode Dawn at home and his presence seemed to have a calming influence on him. He led us out of the paddock as soon as I was in the saddle and Dawn didn't get the chance to get over-excited at all. I cantered down to the start, with Dawn taking a keen but manageable hold, and I started to focus on the race ahead of us.

My instructions were very much the same as before – don't interfere – and when we jumped the first fence in second place very much as before, everything appeared to be going to plan. But then suddenly things didn't seem so straightforward as Dawn jumped slightly to the right over the second fence. I didn't know what to do to keep him straight and as we rounded the sharp left-hand turn for the first time he veered off to the right and we lost several lengths. In the straight Dawn pulled himself into the lead. We were neck and neck with an outsider, Bridge Express. Each time we moved in front of him, we'd come to a turn, lose ground and come out of the corner in second place. We'd take the lead in the next straight and so the pattern repeated itself. As we came round the tight bend the second time we lost the lead to Andrew Wardle on Fellow Countryman. They quickly went five or six lengths ahead and it looked as if Dawn and I would find it hard to catch them. Unlike last time, I was going to have to urge Dawn on long before the last. With each fence we inched closer to the leader and with each corner we lost ground again. The other runners were strung out behind us. Around the final turn Dawn went into top gear and we just got level with Fellow Countryman. He and Andrew Wardle took the inside line and Dawn and I took another three-length detour. We jumped the last fence two lengths behind and despite all Dawn's acceleration went down by a length.

We were led back into the unsaddling area and met by a

very glum-looking fan club. Everyone said 'well done' with false grins on their faces, but I could tell that they all thought we should have won. They were far too kind to say it, but I knew I'd let Dawn down. If only I'd been able to keep him straight we would have won by miles. I know it sounds spoiled to be upset about 'only' coming second, but there's nothing worse in racing than knowing that you have let a good horse down. No matter how much everyone tried to console me, I was convinced that a more experienced jockey would have known what to do. That evening I showed the video to Robert hoping that he'd say there was nothing I could have done, but he confirmed my analysis that the rider was the problem.

I spent the next three weeks replaying the race in my head, trying to work out how I could have got Dawn under control, but all I could conclude was that I needed longer legs! (I'm only five foot two inches.) So by the time I set off for Dawn's third race of the season, at the Beaufort point-to-point in Didmarton, I was much more worried about my ability to control him than about winning itself.

This time the fan club also came with mixed emotions. The Beaufort is one of the most exclusive hunts in the country. This meant better shopping opportunities at the trade stands (good for my mother, less good for my father's chequebook), lots of old friends of my father's from the Army (good for Dad, bad for everyone else). Trickiest of all, the race clashed with the rugby (good for me, very bad for John). Mum, Dad, John, Hils and I arrived to find a course predictably laid out on the side of an exposed, windy hill, with very posh carparking attendants and, joy of joys, a tent with a TV showing the rugby.

The Beaufort course is left-handed but, unlike the South Dorset, it's a real galloping track with long straights and sweeping turns that you only go around one and a half times. Even if Dawn did veer to the right round the corners there simply weren't enough of them to cost him the race.

We were once again entered in the restricted race and there was an enormous field of twenty runners declared to run. The favourite was Lewesdon Hill. He was meant to be ridden by Polly Curling, the reigning champion jockey. Unfortunately, Polly took a crashing fall in the preceding race and Tim Mitchell took her place. Lewesdon Hill had won a maiden and a restricted on his two previous runs at the South Dorset and Hursley Hambledon, and looked a really excellent young point-to-pointer who would be very hard to beat. We were next in the betting followed by General Troy who had been second in his only run of the season, and The Putney Lark who had won his last race impressively. This was an entirely different class of race from our previous two.

My instructions were not to take the lead until the last fence but, as usual, Dawn had other ideas. We started off in the middle of the field, tracking directly behind Lewesdon Hill. Over each fence Dawn came closer and closer to landing on top of Tim Mitchell and his horse. Lewesdon Hill was also taking a firm hold, and by the time we came round the bend into the finishing straight for the first time he was in second place and we were only just tucked in behind in third. Dawn put in another great leap over what would be the last fence next time round and this time landed up besides Lewesdon Hill. At the same time the leader Flaxridge fell, leaving Dawn with nothing but daylight in front of him. That was all the encouragement he needed and he quickly accelerated away from the field.

We set off on the second circuit, bowling along happily with a three-length lead, until we came to a sharp left-hand turn around a flag into the back straight. Dawn refused point-blank to turn left. I pulled hard with my left arm and kicked him in the ribs as forcefully as I could, but Dawn just kept going straight on. The entire field, led by Lewesdon Hill, had come past, taken the corner and were headed towards the next fence when Dawn finally agreed to stop and turn left. We were now some fifteen lengths behind and the commentator announced that we had pulled up and the fan club started to walk back to the lorry. But I couldn't hear the commentary. I was so angry with Dawn that I decided he was at the very least going to jump round the rest of the course. I was furious with him, swore loudly and kicked hard again (not that Dawn seemed to notice my tiny legs). This time he decided to co-operate and we set off at full speed. The faster he went, the better he jumped. He flew over the fences on the back straight as we overtook one after another of the runners and worked our way back into contention. Four fences later we were back with the leading group and, incredibly, by the next fence we were level again with the leader Lewesdon Hill. Storming round the final bend, once more veering to the right, we were just ahead. Any pre-race fear of injury was long gone as I urged Dawn to go as fast as he could into the last fence. He met it right, jumped clear of Lewesdon Hill and won by three-quarters of a length!

That was the day that the West Country racing fraternity began to realise how good Dawn was. Our race was only marginally slower than the Men's Open, and a good five seconds faster than the Ladies' Open, both won by top-class horses who didn't give their competition a fifteen-length head start! As Andy Miller led us back into the winners' enclosure Robert came up to us, didn't say anything to me, but hugged Dawn saying, 'You are one hell of a horse.' Robert didn't say it, but I'm sure he was starting to wonder how long it would be before Dawn joined his professional yard as a 'proper' racehorse. Robert wasn't the only one. Paul Barber (of See More Business fame) asked to buy Dawn in the winners' enclosure; not the time to ask an elated owner-rider to part with her pride and joy really. I just grinned from ear to ear and announced proudly to anyone who'd listen that he wasn't for sale at any price! Old Army friends engulfed Dad, England won the rugby and, although I knew my riding left a lot to be desired, no one questioned my courage or the ability of my horse.

As befits a smart hunt, such as the Beaufort, the owner's prize was an absolutely enormous cup. Unlike most West Country point-to-point courses, the bar actually sold champagne. Armed with both, the whole fan club decamped to the lorry to drink Dawn's health from the cup. By the time we drove home with this huge silver cup on the back ledge of the car, we felt invincible.

After our escapades at the Beaufort, Dawn and I set off for our next race with something of a reputation. Dawn was being talked about as one of the most exciting prospects of the season, even if the girls in the yard had started to call him 'Kitkat' (from 'have a break, have a Kitkat'). I, on the other hand, had a reputation as one of the most disaster-prone owner-riders. As a combination, there was no doubt that we would be exciting to watch.

Our fourth race was at Larkhill in Wiltshire. Larkhill is even more exposed than most point-to-point venues. The course is on the top of Salisbury Plain, effectively in one huge open field beside the Army camp. The fantastic views stretch at least ten miles in all directions and it's not unheard-of for loose horses to gallop off over the horizon after unseating their riders. Unfortunately, the freezing wind blows unimpeded across those miles and chills the onlookers to the bone, and that's on a good day.

Unlike many point-to-point courses, Larkhill is also a semi-permanent racecourse. It has flushing loos in the ladies' changing-room and smart white railings in the finishing straight. Unfortunately, there are no railings as you go out into the country, as Dawn and I found out to our cost.

Unlike maidens, a horse is allowed to win two restricted races before having to graduate to more competitive races. Dawn was odds-on favourite to win our division of the restricted, although there were another fifteen runners for us to beat. The big worry was Woodbury Fair ridden by Mike Felton. Like Dawn, Woodbury Fair was a six-year-old gelding by Over The River. He had been sold the previous year for twenty-five thousand pounds and had won his last race, a maiden, with ease. Racecourse rumour was that Mike Felton was not going to let Dawn and me dominate as we had when we beat him on General Moss, and that he was determined to finish ahead of us.

As ever, the stalwarts of the nascent Cool Dawn fan club were present: Mum, Dad, Hils and John were there to support us. They were joined by my youngest brother Dave on school holidays and Tim, my boss from McKinsey. Tim was over in England on a two-year secondment from Canada. He loved horses and was a keen reader of Dick Francis's novels. He spent much of the afternoon transfixed by the bookies (there is only a Tote in Canada) and by the end of the day he had announced that he was going to have to reread all his Dick Francis books because he now understood what most of the words actually meant. He had been extremely understanding about letting me go racing when I was meant to be working and I was keen to put up a good show for him. Tim joined the rest of the fan club in the paddock and then I fear they all put his new-found knowledge of the bookies into practice.

Harry had told me not to take the lead until the final two fences and to try to keep Dawn surrounded by other horses in order to try and avoid any of the steering problems that we had had at the Beaufort. Dawn took a strong hold but I was just about able to persuade him to stay in third place as we charged towards the first fence. We jumped the first four fences in an uncharacteristically well-controlled manner and we came past the crowd and the finish for the first time still in third place. Larkhill is a right-handed course so we didn't lose ground when Dawn jumped slightly to the right, and the railings in the finishing straight kept him on a good line as we set off on the final circuit. As we headed downhill away from the crowd, Dawn started to accelerate and gain ground on the leaders so that we were a clear second when we approached the eleventh fence. The third horse was at least two lengths behind us. We were not as well surrounded as Harry had hoped. Three strides from the fence, with absolutely no advance warning, Dawn tried to avoid jumping the fence, ran out to the right and headed for the wide expanses of Salisbury Plain. I don't know if a more experienced rider could have stopped him. He was always pretty determined. But I had no chance, and that was that, we were out of the race. The rest of the field jumped the eleventh and galloped on, leaving Dawn and me with a long walk home.

To add insult to injury, as I trotted Dawn back, he bucked me off and stood staring at me as I pulled myself out of the mud. There was no question about who was in charge of this relationship. In the distance I could just see Mike Felton and Woodbury Fair come with a late run from the back of the field to win the race with ease. I led Dawn back furious with him and with myself, cursing at the top of my voice. My mother was worried I'd hurt myself and asked Dave to look through his binoculars to see if I was okay. Seeing me swearing like a trooper, he repeated verbatim what he could see me saying and completely shocked Tim with his (and by implication my) language. It was a thoroughly exasperating and humiliating experience and I found it very hard to make polite conversation to the fan club once I had rejoined them in the beer tent to drown our sorrows. This was not what was meant to happen in a Dick Francis story.

And that was where our first season ended. Dawn's back was a little stiff which was what some kind souls said had caused him to run out. We decided to play it safe and give him a rest until next year.

All in all, it had been an incredible spring. It might not have ended on the best note, but two wins and a second out of four runs were still beyond my wildest dreams. Every year, Mackenzie and Selby publish a form guide and summary of the point-to-point season, complete with a description of every horse. In some ways, it's a bit like getting your annual school report. That year, they described Dawn as a 'remarkable youngster' and rated him in the top thirty point-to-pointers in the country. They also described me as a 'complete passenger' and if there had been ratings for jockeys, I'd have been nearer the bottom thirty! But there was nothing they could say that could wipe the smile off my face when I watched the videos of our victories and, fortunately, I didn't have a video of Larkhill to worry about. It wasn't long before I was dreaming of the glory to come next year and with luck the chance to ride Dawn on a proper racecourse in a hunter chase.

Chapter Three

The Second Season

As he had the previous year, Dawn spent the summer of 1994 with my parents at Langport in Somerset. He was turned out with Sammy, and this time Sammy's pony companion Badger stayed with them throughout the summer. Dawn and Sammy had lived happily together the summer before, but it took a few days for the politics of the field to settle down – thanks to Badger. To begin with, Sammy was fiercely defensive of his friendship with Badger and refused to let Dawn get anywhere near the pony. When Dawn did graze near Badger, Sammy bared his teeth and chased him around the field. They were actually living in two fields with a rather thin hedge covering a barbed-wire fence dividing the two. The day after Dawn returned, Mum looked out of the window to see Sammy chase Dawn towards the fence and Dawn fly over it to escape him. At least he hadn't lost his love of jumping.

We no longer had the dreaded horse trailer, so Robert and Sally Alner kindly agreed to come and pick Dawn up on their way back from Taunton races at the end of September and deliver him to Harry Wellstead's yard. They arrived in the early evening to find quite a commotion. My parents had a particularly fierce Jack Russell terrier called Oscar and they were always worried that he would bite visitors. Dad had heard the lorry pull up outside the house and had rushed out to pick Oscar up and stop him from biting the Alners. Oscar didn't like being bossed around at all and had bitten Dad as hard as he could. When Sally rang the bell on the garden gate that was beneath the 'Warning – Dogs! Ring Bell and Wait' sign, she was greeted by Dad with blood pouring from his hand holding a furious, snarling, seething mass of terrier. I know she was quite concerned about what state Dawn might be in.

The only way out of the horses' field that didn't involve trespassing across our neighbour's land, was through a narrow gate into the garden, then across the lawn, down three stone steps and then out of the gate with the bell. Mum fussed about how to get Dawn through this obstacle course, Sally tried to avoid the enthusiastic attentions of my parents' other dogs, while Dad and Oscar growled at each other. It was like something from a Monty Python film. In the midst of all this chaos Robert went into the field, scratched Dawn's ears, and calmly said, 'Hello, old chap.' Then he quietly led him through the narrow gate, across the lawn amidst the fighting people and dogs, and, before anyone else had noticed, Robert had him safely tied up in the horsebox. I think Harry and the Alners were quietly relieved to get Dawn back to Locketts and away from the anarchy at the Harding family home.

By November, just as he had been the previous year, Dawn was ready to hunt. As with the previous year we had to do seven days' hunting to be eligible for a hunters' certificate which would enable us to run in point-to-points and hunter chases. Hunting with Dawn the previous season had been exhilarating, if a bit hairy at times, and I was looking forward to the experience.

Our first day's hunting coincided with the Portman Hunt's opening meet. Together with three other point-to-pointers, also trained by Harry Wellstead, we arrived at Manston, near Sturminster Newton just in time for the meet at quarter to eleven in the morning. Peter, Lucia and Connie, who were riding Harry's other point-to-pointers, all worked in the yard and they were looking forward to a day away from mucking out and grooming. All of us downed the port and sausage rolls that were offered to us with great gusto. As it was the opening meet there was an enormous number of mounted and unmounted followers, and Dawn could sense the excitement and anticipation around him. It looked as if we would have a great fun day out.

Just after eleven o'clock the hounds left the meet and the four of us set off briskly with the rest of the mounted field towards the first draw. The hounds found immediately – it really was shaping up to be a good day – and we galloped across a couple of fields towards a ford across a stream. It had been bucketing with rain all week and the stream, Manston Brook, was bursting its banks. The brook lay between two fields and had barbed-wire fencing on both banks. There were two five-bar gates on either side of the brook, with a ford between them. The sensible hunters were calmly walking through one at a time. Cheered by the port and fresh air, all four of us were gossiping loudly as the point-to-pointers followed each other through the first gate into the water which was up to three feet deep. Dawn had never been in deep water before and as soon as he couldn't see his front feet he panicked and leapt forward colliding with Peter and his horse in front of us. Peter's horse collided with Lucia's, which in turn collided with Connie's. Her mount then leapt sideways slamming the outward gate shut leaving all four of us stuck in the ford. Dawn was having none of this, he whipped around to escape back where he'd come from, tripped and fell off the edge of the ford into yet deeper water. The next thing I can remember is watching the water come over my head as Dawn and I parted company and both went for an unexpected swim. I hauled myself out of the water to be met by an audience of some forty mounted followers on either side of the ford, all roaring with laughter.

I have always dreamt of riding cross-country round

Badminton. Like thousands of others I've watched countless riders fall in the lake there and drag themselves out of the water sopping wet. This culminates with the spectacle of them lying on their backs on the grass with their feet in the air (to drain the water out of their boots), remounting and completing the course. So, without thinking, in front of the entire hunt, I waved my wet legs in the air, drained the water out of my boots and got back into the saddle. Thank goodness that Thelwell (the cartoonist) wasn't there to capture the moment first hand!

Most sensible people would have gone home there and then, but both Dawn and I are more than a little enthusiastic when out hunting and we had really been looking forward to this day. Anyway, whatever I thought, there was no way Dawn could be persuaded to leave the other horses so early in the day. We stayed out for another three hours and only went home when we were faced with the same ford crossing again. This time the new Master and Huntsman of the Portman, Hugo Busby, did a perfect swan dive into the water when his horse stopped dead on the edge of the ford. Dawn and I decided that one swim was quite enough for us so we went home.

Fortunately our other days hunting were less eventful, but I think we would have been granted our hunters' certificate on the basis of that one opening meet alone – for the entertainment value and for fear of what else we might get up to at future meets. Once again, I think the Portman were glad to say farewell to us for another season.

When I bought Dawn my main ambition had been to win a ladies' open point-to-point and maybe ride in a hunter chase. Our initial race of the new season was the first chance I had had of realising one of those ambitions; to win a ladies' open. Dawn was entered in the first ladies' open of the season at Larkhill on 14 January and everyone in the yard thought that we had every chance of winning it.

It wasn't winning, though, that I was thinking about as I

walked the course that morning. All I could think about was what had happened at Larkhill at the end of the previous season. I trudged from fence to fence with grim-faced determination that whatever else happened I wouldn't be so humiliated again. There was no way I was going to let him run out a second time. I bumped into Katie and Tessa Dare, two point-to-point jockeys who had been at school with me, and I don't think they understood why I was so concerned. They thought Dawn was a top-class horse and tried to reassure me that the last time had just been a freak accident. 'What about the Beaufort?' I asked.

'Well, I'm sure he'll have calmed down a bit now he's older,' they replied.

I wasn't convinced.

It seemed a long time since the last race of the previous season, and the fan club had definitely been missing racing. They all turned up with more enthusiasm than is healthy for a point-to-point on a freezing cold hill in January. John had driven down from London with me. Mum and Dad had come up from Somerset, chain-smoking as usual, to control their nerves before a race. Hils was there as ever and had brought her new boyfriend, Hugh, an old friend of mine from Oxford. I had introduced the two of them the year before. Hugh was not a novice to point-to-point following, in fact he had come to watch many of my earlier performances with Sammy years before and briefly witnessed (and profited from) one of my earlier outings with Dawn. At least that meant he knew how many layers of clothing you needed to stay warm at Larkhill in January (as many as you can physically wear). Now married, Georgie Taylor (*née* Dangerfield) could be found complaining that her pregnancy was really getting in the way of her hunting season. She was there to support her father's horse Tubbs as well as Dawn. Robert and Sally Alner weren't racing that day so they had come along to give Harry and me moral support while we all stood in the paddock and reviewed the runners.

The ladies' opens at the beginning of the season tend to have some pretty decent horses in them and this was no exception. There were fourteen runners, but none of them had as high an official rating as Dawn, although several of them were much more reliable and experienced ladies' point-to-pointers. The favourite on the day was Stephen's Pet, ridden by the ex-champion lady rider, Alison Dare. They had won four ladies' opens in a row the previous season, and were definitely the partnership we had to beat. Polly Curling was also in the race on the second favourite, Bond Jnr. He had won a two-mile hurdle the previous season when trained by Paul Nicholls, and word had gone out to the bookies that his new trainer, Richard Barber, rated him very highly. The other fancied partnerships were Qualified, ridden by Lucia Boscowen, who had won three ladies' opens the previous season, and Spacial and Minette Hill who had won two. If Dawn and I were to realise my long-standing ambition we would have to be on top form.

Harry gave me a leg-up and Andy Miller led Dawn and me around the paddock while I tried to get my nerves under control. The first race of the season is always the most nerve-racking. I saw the familiar and statuesque figure of Michael Dangerfield in the crowd and he yelled out 'Good Luck'. Butterflies were whirling round my stomach like a tornado and I was about as far away from carefree and cheerful as it's possible to be but I told myself firmly: 'You claim you do this for fun, so you'd better bloody well smile.' I forced my face into a fake grin and tried hard to look as if I was enjoying myself. I don't think Michael was convinced. Inside, every brain cell I possessed was screaming 'Why do you do this? It's the most dangerous sport in the world – this is insane!' But there was no escaping it now – Andy led us out onto the track and Dawn leapt into a fast canter down to the start.

He pulled hard as we headed downhill to look at the first fence, and it was me who was puffing and out of breath as we arrived. My fitness regime wasn't quite as effective as I might have hoped, but there wasn't much I could do now. I just had to pray that Dawn wouldn't pull too much in the race itself. Ladies' opens tend to go a fair bit faster than mixed races, mainly because the horses carry a stone less weight. In this case, Minette Hill had said that she and Spacial were planning to make the pace. Thankfully this meant that I could aim to keep Dawn behind the leaders till the later stages of the race and hopefully prevent him running out again. My plan was to keep him to the outside with horses in front and inside of him, and not to take the lead till as late as possible – ideally not until the last fence. That way he would always have horses between him and the inside until we got into the finishing straight with its running rails. At least that was the theory.

Before I could ponder my plans any more the race was on. As expected, Minette and Spacial set off in the lead at high speed. Dawn and I were lying fifth coming into the first fence with Polly Curling and Bond Jnr beside us. Dawn measured the fence and sailed over. Bond Jnr on the other hand didn't appear to notice the obstacle at all and crashed into it, somersaulted and sent Polly flying. For a second I was concerned if Polly was all right, but almost immediately the next fence was upon us. Dawn was taking a fair tug on the reins but I was just about able to control him and I wasn't too tired yet. All seemed to be going to plan.

As we came past the crowd and the finish for the first time Spacial was still in the lead with Qualified in second, Stephen's Pet in fifth and Dawn and I were just behind them in sixth. From there the course turns right into a downhill straight where all the horses started to pick up speed into the first two downhill fences and we approached the spot where Dawn had run out the previous season. I was now at my most concerned and beginning to tire. Dawn was pulling very hard and my arm muscles felt that they would snap in two with the strain. Luckily we were on the outside of the leading group, (as I had planned!), with several horses in front of and beside us. There was no way he could run out. He jumped the next fence without a hint of what had happened the year before. As I felt the relief of avoiding last year's disaster Dawn started pulling harder and harder and my arm muscles were approaching exhaustion. Dawn took full advantage of my weakening grip and started to accelerate. We were now lying in third with only Qualified and Spacial ahead of us. Flying over the open ditch Dawn gained another length and as we approached the last downhill fence we drew level with the leaders. Without so many horses around him Dawn thought about running out – I could feel him leaning to the right – but something must have changed his mind because he sailed over and went one length ahead. My arms were totally dead. As soon as Dawn saw daylight ahead of him he started to pull even harder and I had no strength left to fight him. We went into the dip at the bottom of the course and disappeared from the sight of the spectators a length ahead of Spacial and Qualified. By the time we reappeared into the view of the crowd, turning for home up a gradual incline we were some four lengths ahead and still accelerating. I heard Minette yell to Lucia and Alison: 'Don't worry – she can't hold him. I'm sure he'll come back to us when he tires.' She was right about me, but she didn't know Dawn.

We approached what had been the first fence clearly in the lead. With only four fences to go, Minette, Lucia and Alison started to wonder if they had let us get too far in front. Dawn was bowling along happily now I wasn't fighting him for control. We jumped the next two fences well and were still three lengths ahead going into the second last. We met it wrong and Dawn took off a stride too early. For a split second I thought we were about to fall, but I, too, should have known Dawn better. He stretched out his front legs and hardly touched the fence. We rounded the long final bend into the finishing straight clear of trouble, but I could hear the jockeys behind me urging on their horses. I looked around for the favourite, Stephen's Pet, expecting to find him ready to pounce on my shoulder. Stephen's Pet was some ten lengths behind me in third and even the second horse, Qualified, didn't look like he was getting any closer. I could hardly believe it, we were going to win a ladies' open. I didn't push Dawn on yet, because we still had one fence to jump and it would be just my style to fall at the last. But, as ever, Dawn had things under control. He measured the last perfectly and crossed the line six lengths ahead of Qualified and Lucia Boscowen without having really been challenged. We had won our first ladies' open!

Andy Miller led Dawn and me into the winners' enclosure to find a jubilant fan club. Everyone was ecstatic that Dawn had won and that I had almost seemed in control. It was a far cry from the Larkhill experience only ten months earlier. I couldn't have been more happy. I had hoped that we would win a ladies' open at some stage in the season, but to win a really competitive ladies' open in only our fifth race together was out of this world. John and I drove back to London gleefully reliving the race stride by stride.

Having achieved the first part of my ambition for Dawn, I was now keen to complete the second and ride him in a hunter chase. Unfortunately, there weren't any suitable hunter chases in the immediate future so just three weeks later we all found ourselves back at Larkhill for the New Forest point-to-point. Dawn was entered in both the Mixed Open and the Point-to-Point Owners Association (PPOA) Race. The plan was to run in whichever looked the least competitive on the day.

Unlike racing under rules where runners are declared the day before, in point-to-points you have until thirty-five minutes before the race to decide whether you are going to run or not. I spent a very nerve-racking hour waiting outside the secretary's hut marking off each of the runners as they were declared. With ten minutes to go before the close of declarations for the Mixed Open, Harry and I reviewed the runners. The Mixed Open was looking very competitive with two very strong Richard Barber horses declared – Fosbury and Tricksome – not to mention Qualified, who we had beaten last time, and Tubbs owned by Michael Dangerfield. The PPOA was nothing like as competitive so we decided to sit out the Mixed Open and wait for the later PPOA race.

Forty-five minutes later Lucia Boscowen and Qualified trotted up the easy winners of the Mixed Open and I began to worry that we had made the wrong decision. Dawn and I had beaten them equally easily three weeks before, so we surely would have beaten them again. This was a completely new type of stress. I was already wound up with my usual fear of hurting myself and the terror of letting Dawn down. Now I could worry about race selection as well. Just why did I choose to spend my weekends in this state of nerves? As usual before a race, I was not exactly thinking rationally.

An hour later there was no point in worrying about race selection because I was walking into the paddock to greet the fan club. Hils and Hugh, my parents and Georgina were there as before, but this time John had had to stay in London for a business meeting. I was convinced that as he wasn't at Larkhill I was bound to hurt myself.

As it turned out, the field for the PPOA race was definitely weaker than the Open. So much weaker that Dawn was the 5–2 odds-on favourite. The second favourite was Sorrel Hill, ridden by a top West Country jockey, Shirley Vickery. They had won three point-to-points the previous season and looked to be a pretty decent combination. The only other serious competition came from Carly's Castle who had won five out of her last eleven races. The other five runners didn't have anything like Dawn's form.

I cantered Dawn down to the start with much more confidence than I had had three weeks before. Again my big worries were preventing him from running out and trying to keep him from taking the lead too early, but I had managed it last time, so with luck I could do it again.

With only seven runners we didn't circle at the start for

long. The starter dropped his flag and once again I braced myself for Dawn to start to pull my arms out of their sockets. Unfortunately, there wasn't the strong pace that there had been in our last race and I had much more trouble keeping Dawn behind the leaders. Shirley Vickery took up the lead at the second fence but Dawn and I weren't far behind in third. Over the fourth fence Edge of the Glen made an awful mistake and catapulted his jockey Malcolm Batters into the ground. That left six of us. As we came past the crowd I was narrowly winning the battle of control with Dawn and we were in fourth place just two lengths behind the leaders. But we weren't going fast enough for Dawn to settle and I wasn't going to be able to hang on for much longer. We headed downhill and Dawn started to make up ground. I was just able to keep him on the outside as we approached the point where he had run out before, but we were now lying second and only a length behind the leader. He didn't make any attempt to run out. We jumped the open ditch easily, gained another length and were in the lead as we approached the last fence in the downhill straight. Just where we had taken the lead in our last race.

My arms were running out of strength but Dawn jumped the fence perfectly then gave another big tug of the reins. Once more I admitted defeat and let him run on at his own pace. We disappeared out of sight from the crowd and accelerated away from the field. Coming past what had been the start I couldn't hear any horses behind me at all, only the wind whistling in my ears. I looked round to see that Shirley Vickery and Sorrell Hill were a couple of lengths behind us with the rest a long way back. I could see that Shirley was starting to close on us so I gave Dawn a couple of quick kicks in the ribs. He wasn't used to me issuing instructions but he was always happy to go a bit faster and he willingly accelerated away from Sorrell Hill.

We were now approaching the second last but, just in time, I saw that we were being directed around the outside of it.

Malcolm Batters was still being treated by the medical team on the other side of the fence – another all too timely reminder of the dangers of my chosen sport. But despite the dangers there was still a race to win. I urged Dawn on just in case Sorrell Hill was closing on us. But Dawn's burst of acceleration had been too much for Sorrell Hill and we rounded the final bend alone, a good fifteen lengths in front and still going away. We jumped the last well under control and crossed the finishing line with a winning margin of twenty lengths. That was two races in a row that we had won without any form of unexpected mishaps at all. I felt like a proper jockey!

Once again everyone in the fan club was bubbling with excitement. They agreed with me that I did look as if I had finally got Dawn under control. Only Hugh was a bit unhappy, with our odds of 5–2 on, as there was not much return for his betting. He, like a number of followers, wanted to see Dawn run with odds where it was worth while backing us, or at least where the bookies thought another horse stood a chance of beating us!

The next day I took the video over to Locketts for Robert to see, expecting him to agree with Dawn's fan club's view of my improved style. Unfortunately, he proved a harder task master. While he couldn't argue with the fact that we'd improved since the Beaufort, he still felt that I was leaning back too much over the fences and not sitting low and still enough in the saddle. There was clearly much work still to do on my style.

There was another reason that I needed Robert to endorse my riding. I was desperately hoping that Dawn and I could try our hand in a hunter chase. To do that I needed to get a permit from the Jockey Club to ride on a proper racecourse in amateur-only races. Getting a permit required me to obtain references from two professional trainers saying that I was a competent jockey. I already had one reference from a Yorkshire-based trainer called Tom Tate for whom I had ridden out during the winter while working on a consulting assignment in Leeds. But Tom had not seen me jump anything. Robert was very impressed with Dawn's performance in the video, and I think he felt that Dawn deserved his chance in hunter chase even if he wasn't sure about me. He agreed to give me the reference, and I was free to dream about fulfilling my ambition of riding in a hunter chase.

The only other thing I needed to do was get some new colours. The point-to-point colours that Mum had knitted for me many years before were not allowed on a proper racecourse. The white zig-zag stripe down the middle wasn't one of the styles that the Jockey Club allowed so I had to get some much more traditional colours made. Conveniently, no one else had registered a blue body with white sleeves and a thick white stripe down the middle so at least my proper colours weren't too far off my point-to-point ones.

In the middle of February I resigned from my job as a management consultant at McKinsey and Company. With two weeks' holiday before starting my new role as Marketing Director at Thomas Cook, I headed off to Locketts for a week riding out with the string. I was totally dedicated to improving my style in anticipation of my first ride in a hunter chase. That ride was planned for the second week of my holiday at a Wednesday meeting at Folkestone.

As I was spending my holiday down in Dorset I hitched a lift with Dawn in the lorry. Folkestone racecourse is a good five-hour journey from Locketts by lorry – which is about four and a half hours too long if you are terrified about what meets you at the other end. The lads tried to distract me, but as we got closer and closer to Folkestone I got more and more grey and silent with nerves. I had bought Dawn, hoping that one day I would ride him on a professional racecourse, but somehow that had always seemed part of a very hopeful dream. Now that the impossible dream was getting very close indeed to being reality, I was starting to have major second thoughts. Riding in front of a small crowd at Larkhill is one thing; seeing your name in the national papers on the racing page and knowing that people in betting shops all around the country will be watching you with their money at stake was quite another thing. I was convinced that I would do something disastrously wrong – like fall off going down to the start. Even if I got as far as the race itself everyone had told me that fences on professional courses were much bigger and less forgiving than point-to-point fences. I was in quite a state of nerves by the time the lorry pulled in to the racecourse.

My grey face was a good match for Folkestone racecourse that day. The course is only a mile or so from the sea on an exposed open area just beside the motorway. It isn't a flashy or smart course, in fact the stands feel rather like an old seaside pier that has probably seen better days. There was a howling gale blowing off the Channel and large storm clouds were charging across the sky. The atmosphere was bleak, the light was grey and it was starting to rain really quite miserably. I should have been reassured that at least the weather was reminiscent of point-to-pointing, instead I had a sense of foreboding that the grey weather was a symbol of what was to come.

I took my kit over to the weighing-room and was immediately struck by the difference in routine from point-to-pointing. Little things were different for no apparent reason. For example: when you weigh out before a point-to-point you include the weight of the number cloth. In proper racing you don't. At a point-to-point the owner signs a form saying that the horse has arrived and is going to run. On a proper racecourse the trainer signs it instead. All these little differences were guaranteed to make me feel out of place.

The fan club also found some small differences between professional racing and point-to-pointing. The main one was that midweek racing was simply not as easy to support as weekend point-to-pointing. Most of the fan club couldn't take the day off – including John. It was only Mum, Dad and Hils who made it to Folkestone. The only positive improvements they could find were warm coffee and shelter. They took refuge from the gathering storm in the owners' and trainers' bar and loudly extolled the value of hot drinks and a roof over their head as infinitely preferable to a flask of lukewarm coffee consumed in a muddy field. At least they were starting to feel like they belonged.

As I came out of the weighing-room, I saw Jamie Osborne and Richard Dunwoody – two of the leading professional jockeys – and I couldn't believe that I would be riding at the same meeting as them. I wanted to get their autographs but I thought that it wasn't really appropriate if I was a fellow jockey!

I walked the course with Peter Henley who was riding one of Robert's runners that day. Peter was an amateur like me, but that's where the similarities between us ended. He was one of the season's top amateurs and hoped to be good enough to turn professional in the near future. He had ridden round Folkestone several times before, and kindly talked me through the idiosyncrasies of the course. Folkestone is a right-handed track in a fairly regular oval shape. The turns aren't too tight and although the fences seemed big to me, Peter assured me that they were relatively easy for proper national hunt obstacles. Our race was over two miles and five furlongs and we would do two circuits of the course. The going was very heavy and we could hear the ground squelching under our feet as we walked round. Out on the racecourse it didn't seem too different from a point-to-point course, after all I found point-to-point courses scary to walk anyway, and by the time Peter and I got back I had just about managed to get my nerves under control.

I took myself off to change and was delighted to find not one but two other lady jockeys to keep me company. Jane Cobden was riding her mother's horse, Mr Golightly, and Nicky Ledger was riding Rusty Rails. There were six other horses in our race, all with male jockeys. Of all of them our main danger was Mr Golightly. He was a really lovely horse and he and Jane had been placed in three hunter chases the season before. Jane and I had been at school together at Leweston and it was nice to have a friendly face to chat to in the changing-rooms, but we both knew that it would be a different matter once we got on to the course. The other dangers appeared to be Linred, ridden by Tim McCarthy, and St Laycar, ridden by Alan Greig. The former had been second in his last point-to-point and looked a decent horse, while the latter had been placed in hunter chases the previous season.

While I was waiting in the ladies' changing-room thinking about how close I was to realising my ambitions or failing in the pursuit of them, Dawn was also coming to terms with the differences from point-to-pointing. In point-to-points the horses are usually saddled up in their own horseboxes and brought down to the paddock only once they are fully tacked up. On a proper course the horses are taken to the pre-parade ring at least half an hour before their race and before they have been saddled up. The trainer collects the saddle from the weighing-room and then the horses are saddled up in open-sided stalls where the public can watch. Dawn didn't think much of the saddling arrangements. Andy led him into one of the saddling stalls and he immediately started kicking out. He would not stand still to be saddled at all. When he tried to rear up and narrowly missed banging his head on the roof of the stall, Andy gave up and led him round the back of the stall so he could be saddled out of sight from the public.

The rain was lashing down and the wind was whistling through the stands – it really wasn't a nice day for racing. Mum, Dad and Hils had been quite reluctant to come out of the nice warm sheltered bar, but it wouldn't be racing without the Cool Dawn fan club and I walked into the paddock to find the three of them, plus Harry, huddled together, braced against the wind.

My instructions were to try and hold on to Dawn's head

and not let him take the lead until the second circuit at the earliest, but I wasn't thinking about that as we cantered down to the start. For once I also wasn't thinking about being run away with either. Dawn and I cantered past the stands and all I could think about was that now I had reached the absolute pinnacle of my racing ambition. As we circled round at the start I made myself look up at the rather battered facade of Folkestone stand and tried to commit the scene to memory. It may have been bucketing down with rain but that didn't matter to me – Dawn and I were about to start our first hunter chase.

We lined up for the start and once again I was very conscious of the differences from our previous races. In a point-to-point all the horses get in a vague line along the course, the starter stands on a little ladder with a flag in the air and drops his flag to indicate that you should start. All this happens on a proper course, but there is also a thick rubber tape that is stretched across the course which prevents any horse from setting off until the starter is ready. The starter drops his flag and also pulls a lever that frees the rubber tape and leaves the way clear for the horses to set off. Dawn and I had never seen this sort of starting contraption before, and we were both taken by surprise by the loud 'pinging' sound the tape made as it rushed back across the course. For a split second both Dawn and I froze and watched it and then we were off.

That split second was all it took for the other horses to get ahead of us. Mr Golightly and Jane took the lead as they landed over the first fence while Dawn and I were about four lengths behind them in fourth. At the third Linred unseated his rider and Dawn and I were starting to get back in touch with the leader – still Mr Golightly. As we came past the stand the first time Dawn and I were a clear second and we had Mr Golightly in our sights some eight lengths in front. I was concentrating so hard I didn't really notice the rain but there was no doubt that Dawn did. He didn't like the heavy ground at all and was not pulling as much as I was used to. We headed away from the stands on the final circuit and as we turned into the back straight I could hear and feel the strong headwind as if I were being kicked in the chest. I urged Dawn on towards the next, plain fence but he misjudged it and hit it hard with his front legs. I was catapulted forward and landed on his neck far too close to his ears for comfort. I knew I would inevitably fall off if he dropped his head, but he seemed to realise that I was perched up too high and let me push myself back into the saddle. We had lost a lot of ground and Mr Golightly was now some twelve lengths ahead of us. Jane was really stretching the field.

There was no sign of the other runners; Dawn and I were a good twenty lengths ahead of the third horse who was about the same amount ahead of the next. I gathered up my reins and nervously encouraged Dawn towards the next fence. We couldn't afford another mistake. He jumped it beautifully this time but we had a lot of ground to make up and nobody for company as we battled against the wind. Around the final bend I thought we were catching Mr Golightly but Jane must have been giving her horse a breather. The mud was really deep as we entered the finishing straight and there was nothing we could do when Jane kicked her horse forward for one last effort. They were now nearly fifteen lengths ahead of us. Mr Golightly met the last wrong and Jane almost came off but she clung on just as I had earlier. Dawn and I were well and truly beaten in second.

I should have been ecstatic about coming second in my first proper race but I never enjoyed being beaten and Folkestone was no exception. I was really pleased that Jane had won her first hunter chase and quite chuffed with my own three hundred and fifty pounds of prize money (nearly four times what we had won in our last point-to-point!). But I also felt it could have been much closer if I had ridden better. Harry tried to cheer me up by saying that Dawn obviously hadn't enjoyed the ground, but I was not pleased with my performance. I had let Dawn get far too far behind Mr Golightly at the start so he always had too much ground to make up. What's more I had very nearly fallen off. I spent the next few hours replaying my mistakes in my head but whatever I did there was no way I could change the result of the race. The drive home from Folkestone in ever-worsening wind and rain seemed even longer than the tortuous journey there.

Dawn had run in three races in just over a month so we decided to give him a bit of a break before his next race. I had a new job to get to grips with, so it wasn't until a month later that we entered for another hunter chase; this time at Lingfield. The race was on a Friday and I explained to my boss at Thomas Cook, Nigel Hards, that I would work from home in the morning and then take the afternoon off to go racing. I don't think Thomas Cook had ever had an amateur jockey as an employee before, let alone as their Marketing Director, but Nigel was very understanding and only really wanted to know if he should put a bet on. This was something I never advised my friends – and especially not my boss – to do.

Lingfield is pretty much due south of London. I decided to take the train from Victoria rather than do battle with the South Circular road and all the nightmare traffic. I sat on the train with butterflies multiplying in my stomach and worried that I would be late. I had plenty of time, in fact racing wasn't due to start for another couple of hours, but I was worried about how long the walk might be from the station to the racecourse itself. It was a clear, fine and chilly day as I stared out of the window at beautiful green fields that were still recovering from fierce storms over the previous few days. There was plenty of standing water in the fields and it looked as if we would be facing heavy ground again.

The train arrived at Lingfield station and I was surprised to find that I was the only person going racing on the train that day. It seemed a bit odd, but then it didn't surprise me that midweek racing on a cold February afternoon wasn't overly popular, and I was very early. It was only a short five-minute walk to the course and I went off to find the ladies' changing-room. The course was very empty, in fact I couldn't find a soul in the weighing-room. And then it suddenly hit me: racing must have been called off. It had never occurred to me to check in the morning, but all that standing water I'd seen from the train must have left the course waterlogged. I finally found someone cleaning one of the restaurants who confirmed my suspicions: there had been an inspection at eight o'clock in the morning and the meeting had been abandoned. Apparently the news had been on Ceefax from eight-thirty that morning. I felt very foolish.

I was crossing the road behind the stands and heading back towards the station with my tail between my legs when I heard a car hooting its horn at me. It was my parents. They had just arrived from Somerset – a mere three-hour drive away – and were bubbling with excitement about the day's racing ahead of them. I broke the bad news and they wouldn't believe me at first. They had a look at the completely empty carpark and soon they too realised how stupid we had all been. Fortunately, Harry and Andy were more experienced and they and Dawn had never even left Locketts. As it was a Friday, none of the fan club had been able to make it, just as well really! Mum and Dad grimly turned the car round and set off on a three-hour return journey and I trudged back to the station. All three of us had learnt an important lesson about National Hunt racing: always check Ceefax before leaving home, there is no predicting the English weather.

Fortunately, we didn't have long to wait for Dawn's next race. Just in case the Lingfield hunter chase was cancelled, Harry had sensibly entered him in a point-to-point the following day. There weren't many hunter chases for Dawn in the next week or two so we decided we might as well run, and the next day we all set off for Larkhill once again.

Dawn was entered in the Mixed Open. There were five other runners with only one real danger – Polly Curling and Clandon Jack. Clandon Jack was a decent horse trained by Richard Barber and had won three out of his four starts the previous season. He had won his first race that season so easily that the second horse was nearly two fences behind him. Polly was riding at the top of her form and could never be ignored. Nonetheless Dawn's previous two performances at Larkhill had been very impressive and the punters clearly thought we should win – we were 4–6 odds-on favourite.

After Folkestone it was nice to be in the familiar world of point-to-pointing. Both Dawn and I were much more at home with the saddling arrangements and I would almost say I was calm when Harry legged me up into the saddle. Almost. The fan club, particularly my parents, were also pleased to be point-to-pointing again, though there was an occasional mutter about the benefits of hot coffee and shelter from Hils.

Dawn took his usual strong hold – I would almost have been worried if he hadn't – and was alert and happy as we circled down at the start. The sun was just starting to break through the usual grey English sky and Dawn's coat was glistening in the bright light. He really did look like a top-class horse. Polly looked at him and said, with a tinge of envy, how well he looked and then warned me to stay clear of her over the first few fences. Clandon Jack took a ferociously strong hold and she was worried that if I couldn't hold Dawn the two of us would have a ding-dong battle for the lead over the first few fences and destroy both our chances. I was not at all sure that I would be able to hold Dawn but our instructions were to try not to take the lead till the last three fences so I was happy to oblige Polly as best I could.

In fact, Clandon Jack's style of racing suited Dawn and me just fine. He set off in the lead at a tremendously fast pace. So fast that I was able to keep Dawn back in third place without our usual tug of war. We came past the crowd with Polly and Clandon Jack some six lengths in the lead with the field well strung out. Dawn was going easily in third and I hoped we would be able to make up some ground as we turned downhill away from the finishing straight. Downhill we jumped into second place and approached the dreaded corner where we had run out previously with no horses between us and the inside of the track. Fortunately, Dawn seemed to have grown out of his bad behaviour and we jumped the next two fences safely in second place, gaining ground on Polly with every fence. Into the dip and out of sight of the crowd we were still in second, but now only a length behind Polly, with the other runners at least twelve lengths behind us both. As predicted, it had become a two-horse race.

Polly jumped the first fence in the long home straight slightly in front of us. Dawn still had plenty of running in him and as we quickened away from the fence I urged him on. We were quickly level with Clandon Jack and jumped the next fence side by side. Dawn gained a length in the air and that was the last we saw of our competition. Dawn quickened up again and we were soon some five, then a clear ten lengths ahead. I was starting to really enjoy myself. Dawn felt so sure of himself that the only real danger was that I would get complacent and stop concentrating. We still had to negotiate the remaining three fences. We jumped the last open ditch with ease, then the next and rounded the final bend by now a good twenty lengths in front. I was worried Dawn wasn't concentrating any more, so I slapped him down the neck and kicked him into the final fence. But I should not have worried. He jumped it easily and cantered past the finishing post as the clear winner. As I pulled him up and we turned round to walk back to the winners' enclosure I saw Polly and Clandon Jack jumping the last fence. We had won by the whole length of the run in to the finish.

It was great to be back winning again, and there was no

doubt that Dawn had won very impressively indeed. Almost too impressively, if he could dismiss a decent point-to-pointer like Clandon Jack so easily then it was definitely time to set our sights higher and concentrate on hunter chases. While it was brilliant to win, there was clearly more that Dawn was capable of. Since our first race only just more than a year before, our expectations had changed beyond all belief.

The same was also true for several of the horses running at Larkhill that day. The first division of the restricted race was won by Polly Curling on a young five-year-old called See More Business, who went on to be favourite for the Cheltenham Gold Cup three years later. The next race was won by Hanakham, who went on to Cheltenham to win the staying novices championship, the Sun Alliance Novices Chase, two years later. Hanakham beat one of Dawn's stable mates, Harwell Lad, who was owned by Harry and went on to top National Hunt honours when trained by Robert. All in all, spectators at the New Forest Buckhounds point-to-point that year saw more talented horses than they could ever have imagined at the time.

Buoyed up by Dawn's fantastic performance at Larkhill, I was keen to run him in a premier hunter chase. One of the more valuable novice hunter chases of the season was at Ascot on April Fool's Day. The race was worth a massive five thousand pounds, which meant that roughly half of that went to the winning owner. An utter fortune compared to the ninety-odd pounds you get for winning a point-to-point. It didn't escape my notice that if we won this one race, Dawn would pay for the majority of the season's training fees.

The race was to be held on a Saturday, so the race also had the fan club's vote until Hils and Hugh worked out that they were going to be away skiing. John was on business in America and for a while it looked like he wouldn't be there either, but his plane landed at Heathrow that morning and he came directly from the airport – courtesy of the Virgin Atlantic limousine service. Probably one of the more bizarre destinations they have been asked to go to. Mum and Dad drove up from Somerset – this time after checking Ceefax at least ten times that morning. And we were also joined by one of John's closest friends from university, Alice Findlay.

Alice had never been racing before and she couldn't have picked a better day for it. She met John at Heathrow and joined him in his chauffeur-driven car from the airport. They arrived to find Ascot bathed in brilliant spring sunshine. The white railings of the racecourse were glinting in the sun and it felt hot enough to be July. It was certainly hot enough to dry up the ground – which was good to firm, if not downright hard.

Dawn hitched a lift in the Alner lorry as Robert had a runner that day, but he was not the only point-to-pointer hitchhiking. David Young's horse, Young Brave, came with us too, since he was running in the same race as Dawn. David is the husband of Anne Young who had so deftly facilitated the purchase of Dawn that evening in Ireland with large quantities of best Irish whiskey. David is a barrister in London and, like me, he is mad about National Hunt racing. He had ridden under rules as an amateur and owned several professionally trained horses as well. The season before, Young Brave had been trained by Robert in novice chases, but David had decided to go back to doing things himself and now he was training Young Brave in amateur events. What's more Young Brave was due to be ridden by Michael Miller – the younger brother to Andy who looked after Dawn at the races. Dorset loyalties were definitely going to be divided in our race.

A sunny day's racing at Ascot was very different from windswept Folkestone. No man was allowed into the members' enclosure without a jacket and tie, and many of the women were wearing hats – not wet-weather protection but fashion accessories. Everywhere we turned there were officials in bowler hats guarding the entrances to the different enclosures. When they saw I was carrying a saddle and obviously riding that day they all raised their hats and said, 'Good afternoon Miss Harding – can I carry your saddle?' It all felt very intimidating and definitely a cut above our Folkestone experience.

On arriving, the first thing I did was check out the ladies' changing-room. The room lived up to everything you would expect from 'Royal' Ascot. There was a pristine white linen tablecloth covering a table which was laid out with an enormous variety of drinks and glasses, alongside a hopeful-looking champagne bucket. I was the only lady jockey that day so I also had my very own set of scales and personal loo and shower. The fan club decided that this was all too much for me on my own, so moved in to take advantage of the facilities.

I set off to walk the course with Alice and John, and was very pleased that Robert came with us. He was worried that the ground would be too hard for his runner, Seven of Diamonds, and wanted to test it out first. He had ridden around Ascot himself as an amateur many times and as we walked from fence to fence he explained the challenges of the course to me. Ascot is a right-handed track, about a mile and a half long. Dawn's race was just over three miles, so we would start after the turn away from the stands and race nearly two full circuits. The first three fences are all downhill and the third, the open ditch, was by far the largest steeplechase fence I had ever seen. I am about five foot two and I wasn't tall enough to see over it properly. Robert was confident that Dawn wouldn't find it a problem, but I was left in no doubt that Ascot's fences were of a whole different order of magnitude from Folkestone. Next came the water jump – I had never jumped one before – but again Robert seemed to think it would be no problem. I wished I could be so confident. Then came the long bend called Swinley Bottom, followed by four fences in the back straight. These fences didn't look quite so huge but I could see that they were much stiffer than point-to-point fences. If we made a mistake there would be no chance of brushing through the fence and carrying on, we would certainly fall.

By the time we reached the last two fences in the finishing straight, the second race of the day – a novice chase – was underway. We all stood beside the last fence to watch the runners charge past us. Alice had never been to a proper racecourse before, let alone been so close to the horses in action, and I don't think she could get over quite how fast they travel. The leading two horses took the last at a top speed of some thirty-plus miles an hour and it didn't need much of an imagination to realise how much it would hurt if you fell off. At that stage in the day it wasn't something I really needed reminding of.

Despite the fact that the ground was definitely on the hard side, Robert decided to run his horse and the Cool Dawn fan club piled into the stand to support him. Seven of Diamonds had been a point-to-pointer when Robert was still riding himself, and we all felt a certain sense of loyalty towards Dawn's travelling companion. David Young and his daughter, Yolanda, clearly felt the same way, so the owners' and trainers' stand was full of Dorset amateurs yelling for 'Mickey', as Seven of Diamonds was known at home. Adrian Maguire gave him a superb ride and we all shouted ourselves hoarse as they crossed the line the clear winners. Was it an auspicious start to the day? We all hoped so.

Immediately after the race I took myself off to get changed and weigh out. The ladies' changing-room felt far too smart for me and I couldn't stop myself from worrying that I really didn't belong at this class of racecourse. Once I had changed, I gave my saddle to Harry and stood waiting in the weighing-room with butterflies equipped with polo mallets fluttering round my stomach as usual.

Ascot is so smart that it has two paddocks, one for flat racing in the summer and one for jumping in the winter. The jumping paddock is in front of the stands and a good deal smaller than the flat paddock used for Royal Ascot in June. It is also quite a long walk through the crowd from the weighing-room. There were six other runners in our race and it wasn't long before all six jockeys were trudging through those crowds and I was wondering what on earth I was doing. A few yards before the paddock a small girl jumped out in front of me and asked for my autograph. I didn't think she could really mean me and I explained that I wasn't a professional jockey but I'd be happy to sign her racecard if she really wanted me too. She did, but it all seemed very unreal. Part of me wondered whether the fan club had put her up to it as a practical joke. I arrived to greet the fan club in the paddock looking very bemused. They didn't appear to have set her up, but they all thought it highly amusing and pointed out that I'd better do well to justify this stardom. Whichever way I looked there seemed to be more pressure.

I didn't have much time to take in the beautiful sunny spring day before I was being legged up into the saddle and led out on to the course. I hadn't had much of a chance to evaluate the other runners either, but I knew that Young Brave was our big danger. He was second favourite because, yet again, Dawn and I were favourite at 6–5, just short of being odds on. The next biggest danger was St Laycar who had been third behind us and Mr Golightly at Folkestone. The other four runners didn't have much form between them and it looked to be between the three of us.

Going down to the start, Dawn pulled harder than I had ever known and I began to really worry about keeping to my instructions. I was not meant to take the lead until the second-last fence and to keep Dawn at the back until then. I just managed to stop him in order to show him the first fence before the start and I had very little faith that I would control him for long in the race.

We lined up at the start behind two or three of the other runners. At least this time Dawn and I knew what to expect. Neither of us was surprised when the starting tape whizzed back across the course, in fact Dawn was already pulling hard to be allowed to get going. The course was clear and the horses in front of us leapt into a gallop. Dawn leapt forward as well and I tried to hold him back with all my strength. We were just behind the leading two horses as we took off over the first fence but Dawn was making ground fast. He landed level with the leaders and accelerated away from the fence as fast as he could. There was absolutely nothing I could do about it. Within three strides we were in the lead and I gave up trying to hold him. If I fought him any longer I wouldn't have enough strength to stay in the saddle. The fan club all knew what my instructions were and I think there was a collective groan of 'there goes the plan' from the stand.

We were comfortably in the lead by two lengths as we approached the second fence. Ascot's big downhill fences didn't seem to trouble Dawn and he cleared it with ease. But next came the open ditch. It looked absolutely enormous even from on top of Dawn, and if I had been able to persuade Dawn to refuse it or at least slow down I would have. But there was absolutely nothing I could do except hold on tight and close my eyes. Dawn measured his stride carefully, met the enormous fence spot on and soared over. I opened my eyes again to see the water jump approaching fast. Dawn hadn't seen a water jump before either and we were both rather wary of it. He put in a short stride just in front of it and was a bit ungainly but cleared the fence without touching it and we were still in the lead. We galloped round Swinley Bottom and I had no idea who was behind me. As we jumped the next fence I could hear the second horse behind me as his legs dragged through the top of the fence. They couldn't be that far behind but Dawn was still going easily and happily now he was in the lead and in control. We made the turn into the finishing straight and I could hardly believe that Dawn was going so well. He loved the firm ground and pinged the two fences in front of the crowd with consummate ease. We may not have been following our instructions, but at least we were going well.

We set off away from home on the second circuit happily in the lead, but we had to jump those terrifying downhill fences a second time. As we approached the first downhill fence Young Brave appeared on my outside about half a length behind. Dawn could sense him coming and started to quicken up of his own accord. The last thing I wanted to do was go faster into those big fences but I clearly wasn't making the decisions. Dawn cleared the two plain downhill fences with ease but he was going faster and faster. Young Brave wasn't giving in and was only a length behind us in second, with St Laycar eight lengths behind and the rest some five or six lengths further back. We were now approaching the enormous open ditch and I started to lean back in anticipation of disaster. Dawn was hurtling down the hill and I was convinced I was about to die. He met the ditch wrongly and stood back almost outside the wings. I held my breath but he stretched out his front feet and sailed over the fence. Now I just had the water jump to worry about again. Young Brave had gained ground and was right next to us as we leapt the water, this time a little more fluently than on the first circuit. Dawn was on the inside and managed to go a length clear round the bend and headed on into the back straight. Behind Young Brave the other runners were starting to struggle. It was all down to two Dorset point-to-pointers.

Dawn jumped the four fences in the back straight perfectly and every time he felt Young Brave get closer he accelerated a little bit more. Going around the final bend I allowed myself a tiny thought that we might win, but Young Brave was only a length behind me and I could hear Michael Miller growling at him to encourage him on. This time it wasn't just Dawn who wanted to go faster. I urged him on around the bend trying to do everything possible to win the race. We hurtled towards the second-last fence as fast as we could go, met it right and were still a length ahead coming into the last. By now I had totally forgotten my fear of falling, and winning was all that mattered. I yelled at Dawn and urged him into the last with what was left of my strength. Only a length behind me, Michael Miller was doing exactly the same thing with Young Brave. Dawn cleared the last cleanly and I kicked him on for all I was worth. I could see Young Brave from the corner of my eye, but he wasn't gaining on us and I knew we were going to win. Dawn and I crossed the finishing line three lengths ahead of Young Brave. We had won a hunter chase.

Ascot may have two paddocks, but it only has one winners' enclosure. It was quite something to ride into it on a sunny spring afternoon. The enclosure is to the left and below the main stand so it's almost like an amphitheatre to walk into, with people surrounding you on three sides. Dawn knew he'd done something special and he pricked his ears and raised his head to soak up the applause. All the fan club stood there grinning like the proverbial Cheshire Cat. None of them could quite believe their eyes.

The only remaining challenge facing me was to carry the saddle with its four stone of lead to the scales to be weighed in. I was so elated I fairly bounced along under the saddle (almost half my own body weight) even though some of the Ascot officials clearly found it distressing that they weren't allowed to help me. As soon as we had been pronounced okay by the Clerk of the Scales four men in bowler hats appeared from nowhere and offered to carry my saddle. This really was racing with style!

We all stood in the winners' enclosure for some time soaking up the atmosphere while Dawn had his picture taken. David Young was delighted with Young Brave's performance, even if he hadn't won, so there were no hard feelings between first and second; in fact there was one big Dorset point-to-point party.

Just as we were wondering what to do next, Sir Piers Bengough, Her Majesty's Representative at Ascot, asked if we would all like to have a drink in his box. Sir Piers had been a very successful amateur himself and he had also been in my father's regiment in the army so I think he came close to being an honorary fan club member. He didn't seem to mind that there were quite a lot of us, and we all piled up to his box just along from the royal box. We drank champagne and munched cucumber sandwiches and pinched ourselves to make sure it was all really happening. One of the stewards was in the box and he asked me how many rides I had had under rules. I don't think he believed me when I explained that I had ridden my first winner at Ascot on only my second ride under rules. I'm not surprised he didn't believe me, because I was finding it quite hard to accept as well.

While the Cool Dawn fan club was celebrating, the last race of the day was underway. It was won by High Mind ridden by a little-known jockey called Andrew Thornton. Andrew was riding his first winner at Ascot as well, but we didn't go down and celebrate with him as none of us had even heard of him at that stage. Little did we realise the role he would play in Cool Dawn's next trip to Ascot.

All too soon it was time to leave. We walked down to the stables to bid farewell to Dawn, Young Brave and Seven of Diamonds. Two wins and a second wasn't a bad performance for three current or ex-point-to-pointers from Dorset. I had driven out to Ascot in John's convertible Alfa Romeo Spider, and even though it was only the beginning of April the weather was so good that we drove back into London with the roof down and the Beach Boys blaring at top volume. I'm sure no one in Covent Garden could understand why we were quite so happy.

Dawn was a little stiff after such a tough race on firm ground, and it took a week or so before he was back in full work. It took me every bit of that time to come down to earth. After the non-event at Lingfield everyone at Thomas Cook had been very sceptical about my racing activities, and it was hugely satisfying to be able to go back into work the following Monday and show them the result in the back of the national papers. All my fellow directors were very upset that they hadn't backed us, and immediately decided to have a fiver each on us in our next race.

By the time Dawn was ready for that next race it was nearly the end of the 1995 hunter chase season, but we were all keen to have one more dose of excitement before putting our dreams on hold for the following year's campaign. Dawn was entered in a hunter chase at a Saturday evening meeting at Warwick towards the end of May. The ground was on the firm side, but Dawn seemed to like it and the other entries had nothing like Dawn's rating, so it seemed an obvious target.

John and I were due to get married in the autumn so my mother came up to London the day before the race at Warwick to help me choose a wedding dress. The plan was for Mum and me to drive to Warwick from London, while Dad and my younger brother, Dave, would drive there from Somerset. At the end of the day, Mum would then go back with them to Somerset while I drove back to London.

I was incredibly busy at work and spent the Friday morning in a whirlwind of meetings, e-mails and telephone calls before meeting Mum at two o'clock in the afternoon to visit wedding-dress shops on the Fulham Road. We spent a frantic afternoon charging from one shop to another trying to find a dress that we both liked and could afford. As any bride can attest, this is not an easy combination. Throughout the afternoon my mobile rang constantly with work calls, to the extent that I took at least one call while halfway in and halfway out of a large meringue-like wedding dress. By five we were both completely exhausted and I realised that I hadn't eaten a thing all day. Mum was absolutely furious and threatened to make me withdraw Dawn the next day if I didn't eat something soon.

She sat me down in a small greasy café and made me eat a full, cooked English breakfast. I had to admit that I had been working a bit hard lately. She was concerned that I wouldn't be fit enough to ride the following day, but after things had gone so well at Ascot I was confident that everything would be fine. The truth was that I hadn't had much time to exercise in the previous month because I had been working very late, but I had ridden Dawn five times already that season and hoped that I would have retained enough fitness for just one more race.

Mum was insistent that I was too tired to ride and it didn't help when she got home to find our flat in a total mess with no food or provisions of any kind – she was especially annoyed when she couldn't find any loo paper in the flat either. She insisted that, at the very least, I should avoid driving all the way to Warwick and persuade someone else to give me a lift. John had to go to a stag night and so wasn't coming racing, so the job of chauffeur fell to Hugh. Hils was away and he kindly agreed to drive Mum and me to Warwick and then take me home at the end of the day.

The three of us set off for Warwick at lunchtime on Saturday, all crammed into Hugh's totally unsuitable new sporty Prelude called 'Tarquin'! I must confess I was feeling pretty knackered. I tried to convince myself that the race was only seven minutes long so I must be able to conserve enough energy to do a decent job provided I got plenty of rest beforehand. I spent most of the three-hour journey asleep and felt much refreshed by the time we arrived.

As usual, the first thing I did was walk the course. The course at Warwick is left-handed and somewhat unusual. After the start there are two fences in a line followed by a sharp left-hand turn and a long downhill run of at least three furlongs before the next fence. Then there are six large fences that come quickly, one after another, followed by another bend into the finishing straight and two further obstacles. Our race was three miles and two furlongs so we would do two complete circuits of the track. It's a good thing I didn't have to walk two circuits as after one I was already out of breath – not a good sign at all.

There were only four runners in our race, and Dawn really looked a class above the rest – so long as I could manage the steering. He was the 11–2 odds-on favourite and, by the look of the form, he deserved to be. Of our three opponents one, Rogevic Belle, had not run yet that season and had been sold in February for fourteen hundred pounds. Another, The Merry Gambler, was thirteen years old and hadn't won since winning a bumper five years previously. The third, Evening Rush, had run six times that season and not done better than fourth. None of them had come close to winning a five-thousand-pound hunter chase at Ascot.

I went off to change in the small hut around the corner from the weighing-room that doubled as the ladies' changing-room. It was nothing like as smart as Ascot and seemed to double as the male jockeys' physio room. Rabbett Slattery, the physio, was busy setting up her kit. Fortunately she didn't have any male customers while I was changing, but it certainly gave me something new to worry about!

Harry and his wife Maureen, Robert and Sally Alner and their head girl Kathy, joined Mum, Dad, Hugh and Dave in the paddock. As well as training point-to-pointers, Harry owned a number of horses, some of which had graduated to professional racing. One of them, trained by Robert, had run in the previous race but, unfortunately, its reins had broken after the third fence and it had had to be pulled up. Harry was hoping for better things from Dawn and me.

I wasn't feeling quite as rested as I had hoped, but I was confident that I could sit tight on Dawn for the seven minutes of the race. After our success at Ascot I was no longer expected to hold him up, but instead I was meant to try and settle him so he wasn't fighting me, even if this meant being in front. With the change in tactics I was hopeful that I wouldn't get quite as tired as usual. I was glad that the canter down to the start was quite short because that alone used up most of the strength I had in my arm muscles. I had just got my breath back when the starter called us up to the line and we were off.

Dawn set off at full speed towards the first and we were clearly in the lead as he landed on the other side. So far so good. We took the second in the lead as well, but Dawn jumped to the right and lost a few lengths going into the left-hand bend. This made room for Rogevic Belle to shoot through between us and the rails to go into the lead. Rogevic Belle was pulling even harder than Dawn normally did and quickly went several lengths clear. Dawn was somewhat taken aback by being overtaken and miraculously didn't pull anything like as hard as normal. We set off in pursuit at a decent pace but we weren't closing the gap. I was probably more stressed than I should have been about being behind – memories of leaving Dawn too much to do at Folkestone hadn't yet faded – and I tried to hurry Dawn as we jumped the fences in the back straight.

At this stage the Cool Dawn fan club were all standing in the owners' and trainers' bar watching the race on the TV screen because they couldn't see the back straight from the stands. The bar was full of people who had been drinking for much of the afternoon and tongues were well lubricated with alcohol. Someone a few yards from my mother started making loud and very disparaging comments about my riding. The atmosphere could have been cut with a knife. Mum, puffing furiously on her cigarette, was apparently looking like she was ready to say a few choice words back, while Hugh, spotting the chance of thermonuclear war, wisely stood between the parties. I suspect the atmosphere was almost as tense as the action on the racecourse. Robert and Sally didn't want to say it but they echoed some of the punter's comments; they were increasingly worried about my riding and concerned that I would have a nasty fall at any moment. I was very unbalanced and my attempts to hurry Dawn were making him unbalanced as well.

Dawn had plenty of energy in reserve as we came past the stands some five lengths behind Rogevic Belle, but the truth is I was already exhausted. At the first fence second time around I really wasn't concentrating and I let Evening Rush get half a length in front of us. This is called being 'halflengthed'. The horse half a length behind can be tempted to take off at the same time as the horse in front of him, but because he's that crucial half length further from the fence this often proves too big a jump, and he falls. Dawn did take off too soon, hit the fence but was too good a horse to fall. I clung on with what strength I possessed and the situation in the owners' and trainers' bar got even tenser. Mum and Sally were getting more and more worried about my safety, the unknown angry punter was getting more and more worried about his money. The other inhabitants of the bar had apparently decided to avoid the Cool Dawn fan club and watch the rest of the race elsewhere.

Dawn and I managed to jump the next slightly better and set off down the long hill towards the back straight still some three lengths behind the leader. I pushed him on convinced that we wouldn't catch Rogevic Belle before the finish. We caught up going into the first fence in the back straight but that wasn't enough for me – I was convinced that we needed to be in front and clear as soon as possible or else we wouldn't win. I pushed Dawn into top gear and we jumped the next three fences as fast as I had ever jumped anything in my life. I don't think I can have looked very in control because at this point I think Mum and Sally stopped watching, convinced that it was only a matter of seconds before I fell off. Dawn got the better of Rogevic Belle as we turned into the finishing straight and quickly went several lengths clear as Rogevic Belle dropped to the back of the field and was pulled up.

The other two horses were a long way behind us but I was still worried and we hurtled into the second-last fence at top speed. Dawn got a bit close and hit the fence with his front legs and that was all it took to dislodge me in the saddle. For a second I thought I could hang on, as I had at Folkestone, then all I could see was green grass beneath me and I hit the ground with an almighty thump. I tried to curl up into a ball so the following horses wouldn't trample me. It was several seconds before Evening Rush jumped the fence and now was left clearly in the lead. Another long wait and then The Merry Gambler jumped the fence at least twenty lengths behind in second.

I lay on the ground feeling very sore. I had landed on my backside and it was already starting to hurt, but not as much as my pride. I knew I had let Dawn down badly. I picked myself up and started trudging back towards the stands and I could see a concerned group of Cool Dawn supporters approaching me. Mum and Sally reached me first and they could see I was pretty upset. Harry and Robert had gone to check that Dawn was all right and as soon as Andy had caught him they came to check on me. Robert looked worried but all he said was: 'Now follow me, quickly, and keep your head down.' I wasn't at all sure what he meant but I was too shocked to do anything but obey. I followed him through the gate off the racecourse and back towards the changing-room. Several people in the crowd booed me and someone yelled out 'Useless women jockeys – you shouldn't be allowed to ride.' I quickly realised what Robert had been worried about. Dawn was the odds-on favourite and it was very clear that if I hadn't fallen off he would have won. The punters were angry that I had lost them money and I suddenly remembered that all my fellow Thomas Cook directors had also just lost money on me. It started to sink in what a fool I had been. Robert left me in the ladies' changing-room and told me to get out of my racing kit then people wouldn't recognise me. I did as I was told and tried to come to terms with what had happened. As reality slowly hit home I got more and more miserable. I had let Dawn down but I had also let everyone in the fan club down – and made myself look a complete idiot. The flood-gates opened and I sat in the changing-room and cried my eyes out. Partly it was delayed shock from falling, partly I was upset at not winning – but most of all I felt such an idiot for letting everyone down.

The fan club were very upset but I think I had also scared them rigid. They had all been able to see how tired I was from the beginning and felt it was only a matter of time before disaster struck. Hugh kindly took Mum, Dad and Dave off for a stiff drink, Robert and the Wellsteads went to help Andy look after Dawn and Sally got the short straw of coming to collect me.

I was sitting in a miserable pile of tears and grass-stained breeches when she arrived in the ladies' changing-room and I can't imagine it was a very pretty sight. Sally gave me a hug and a gentle bollocking for not looking after myself. She wouldn't hear a word of my distress at letting everyone down and instead reminded me of all the fun we had had. She was just concerned that I was too tired and stressed in my new job and that that was affecting my riding. In the heat of the moment, in the owners' and trainers' bar, Mum had told Sally that I hadn't eaten anything the previous day and that my flat didn't even contain the basic essentials like loo paper. To my horror this became a bit of a clarion call – for several weeks afterwards when I telephoned Sally the first thing she asked was, 'Do you have any loo paper?' No wonder the fan club had emptied the bar of other punters during the race!

As previously arranged, Mum, Dad and Dave set off for the West Country after the races and Hugh had the pleasure of my company all the way back to London. I was stiff and sore from the fall and completely miserable. Hugh was kind and understanding and pretended not to notice as I sobbed quietly to myself from Warwick to London down the M40.

What I didn't know at the time was that there was another reason why Hugh was so quiet. That morning, he had decided that it had been far too long since Dawn and I had had a disaster on the racecourse. He had convinced himself that by the sheer law of averages it was highly likely that Dawn and I would not complete the race and he had put a big bet on Evening Rush to win. Hugh (and my little brother) had made a complete packet on my fall. Sensibly he was convinced that I, and the rest of the fan club, would lynch him for being disloyal. It was only when I told him I planned to write a book, three years later, that he confessed!

Our Warwick race was in early May, only a month before the end of the hunter chase season. Harry would not consider running Dawn again on the grounds that I wasn't fit enough, so that was the end of our second season. Rather like the first season we had ridden an incredible roller-coaster. From the highs of Ascot to the dismal lows of Warwick, once again we had achieved more than I could ever have imagined. We had won a ladies' open, as I had hoped, and not only completed two hunter chases but actually won one at Ascot. If only I could pretend that Warwick hadn't happened.

Those respected voices of the racing intelligentsia, Mackenzie and Selby, viewed our second season in much the same terms as our first. Again they were extravagant in their praise for Dawn describing him as 'top class without a doubt'. But they were even more damning in their criticism of me, saying that 'Dido Harding remains a complete passenger, and all [Dawn's] defeats are probably down to her.' I tried to take their comments on the chin, because after Warwick I knew they were probably right, but there was one thing that stopped me getting too depressed. They rated Dawn as one of the top fifteen hunter chasers in the country. He was no longer eligible for novice hunter chases and if he was really that good then he deserved to run in the top open hunter chases of the season. The top hunter chase of the year was the Cheltenham Foxhunters, run immediately after the Gold Cup. If Dawn was genuinely one of the country's top hunters then it was not unreasonable to believe he and I could run at Cheltenham. That was certainly worth daydreaming about through the summer.

Chapter Four

Dreaming of Cheltenham

It took long into the summer before my pride had recovered from the disaster at Warwick. By the time Cool Dawn came back from his summer holiday to resume work, I had faced up to one important criticism: I just wasn't fit enough. My new job with Thomas Cook was based in Peterborough and as John was still working in central London I spent one and a half hours each morning and evening on the train, commuting between our Covent Garden flat and my office. This left me little time to go to the gym in the evening, let alone to ride. If I was going to partner Dawn at Cheltenham I couldn't afford to be out of breath and holding on for dear life over the last fence – always assuming that I was even fit enough to get to the last fence.

John had been very keen on rowing at university and he was convinced that a lot of the muscle groups used for rowing were the same as race-riding, so in September we swallowed hard and spent eight hundred pounds on a rowing machine. The rowing machine was installed in our spare room, complete with an old TV and video so that I could watch inspirational videos of our past races while puffing away. There was no doubt that, just like horses who work harder when they are enjoying themselves, my rowing was much improved by watching a recording of the previous year's Cheltenham Foxhunters, all the time dreaming that

Dawn and I were there. I would love to be able to write that every evening I toiled away for forty-five minutes. The reality was more like twenty minutes every two days, but at least it was a start.

As usual, Dawn had to start the season with seven days' hunting with the Portman, but unlike previous years I don't have any exciting tales to relate because I wasn't there for all but one or two of his days out hunting. On 28 October John and I were married and we spent the majority of November away on our honeymoon. While we were away Robert kindly agreed to hunt Dawn for me. Robert claims that they had several uneventful days hunting and no one from the Portman has ever been indiscreet enough to contradict him, but I have a feeling that Robert has never jumped fences out hunting faster than he did on Dawn. Certainly Dawn did something to impress him, as after Christmas he suggested that he should train Dawn for the forthcoming season rather than Harry. Robert's professional yard was going from strength to strength and we all thought it would do Dawn good to work regularly with higher-quality horses. The only downside was that we wouldn't be able to run in point-to-points if he joined a professional yard. As he had already proved that he was capable of winning hunter chases, and we were all hoping that he would be running in the very top hunter chases, it didn't seem too big a risk to take. So it was decided: we'd aim for hunter chases only from Robert's yard and possibly have a shot at Cheltenham if we were good enough.

Cheltenham cast a big shadow over our preparations in January. The Cheltenham Festival is held every year in the middle of March and is the Olympic Games of steeplechasing. There are three days of championship races that are the absolute pinnacle of jump-racing achievement. On the last day of the Festival there are two races over three miles and two furlongs: the Cheltenham Gold Cup and the Cheltenham Foxhunters. The former is the most prestigious race for professional horses and jockeys and the latter is the equivalent for hunter chasers with amateur jockeys. Most amateurs dream of having a horse good enough to ride at the Cheltenham Festival. In all the years of plodding around at the back of point-to-point fields on Sammy, it had never crossed my mind that I would have a horse capable of running in the Foxhunters, but that didn't stop me from appreciating just how special and exciting it would be. If Dawn and I could reproduce our Ascot performance we could justifiably enter for the Foxhunters, but first we had to put Warwick behind us and prove that that was just a one-off bad day.

Our first race of the season was planned for Sandown on a Thursday at the beginning of February. But not for the first or last time, my business life clashed with racing. At Thomas Cook we had our weekly directors' meeting every Thursday morning at half past eight. As February is one of the busiest times of the year for the travel trade I was keen not to miss the most important decision-making meeting of the week. Equally, there was no way I was going to miss Dawn's first race of the season. So I took the seven o'clock train up to Peterborough carrying all my racing gear, expecting to attend the meeting and then take the train back to London and on to Sandown a couple of hours later.

The first race of the season is always nerve-racking and this year was no exception. I sat on the early-morning train feeling sick with nerves and trying to force-feed myself a British Rail cooked breakfast to give me energy. There was no way I was going to repeat what had happened before Warwick! I don't think I was concentrating very hard during the directors' meeting that morning but halfway through my boss interrupted us with an urgent message for me. Sandown had been called off because of overnight frost and he'd just seen it on Ceefax. It appeared that he was now a fully-fledged member of the Cool Dawn fan club and had been checking out our competition before placing a bet. The cooked breakfast was still sitting rather uneasily on my stomach and it took most of the morning for me to calm down again and focus on work for the rest of the day. Fortunately, this time my parents had also thought to check Ceefax so there was no repeat of our journey to an empty and deserted Lingfield, but it was still a bit of an anticlimax.

We had a three-week wait before there was another hunter chase that suited Dawn. This time the race was at Kempton and it looked like being one of the most competitive hunter chases ever. Proud Sun, the ante-post favourite, was the top novice hunter chaser of the previous season and definitely one of the major contenders for Cheltenham. The field also included Teaplanter, another top-class hunter who had been second in two Foxhunters. There were another nine runners who all had decent hunter chase form. Robert was adamant that we shouldn't run in the Foxhunters unless Dawn and I had put Warwick firmly behind us and proved ourselves capable of giving the very best hunters a run for their money. As there were just three weeks until Cheltenham, this was likely to be our only chance to book a ticket to the Fox-hunters. We needed to finish in the first three at the very least.

I had the good sense to avoid the British Rail breakfast that morning, but I still felt sick with nerves as I arrived at Kempton. It seemed that the only thing worse than being at Warwick had been not being there and instead seeing my fall in a bookies. So even though Kempton was on a Friday the fan club turned out in force. Mum and Dad were almost as nervous as me for the first race of the season. They had given up smoking as a New Year's resolution but one glance at the large Kempton fences had both of them reaching for the cigarettes they had bought especially on the drive up from Somerset. Hils took the day off to join us, as did John, and Georgie drove up from Dorset armed with her camera. We were joined for the day by a new fan club member, Laurence Tarlo. Laurence and his wife Barbara had bought the manor house next door to Locketts and had shares in a couple of horses trained by Robert.

Robert and I walked the course together to discuss tactics. Kempton is a right-handed, flat and triangular-shaped course which is about a mile and a half long. We would do two complete circuits in our three-mile race. The fences were nothing like as big as Ascot's and were much more evenly spaced than Warwick's. Robert told me to forget about Warwick completely and try and do exactly what we had done at Ascot. He said I shouldn't worry if Dawn jumped to the front, but instead I was to try and get him to settle down and stop pulling once in front. It all sounded very straight-forward in theory, but there was no way I could forget about our experiences at Warwick. I trudged from fence to fence trying to listen to Robert's sound advice rather than the nagging doubts in the back of my mind, but most of the time my doubts seemed to be on loudspeaker. How was I going to avoid falling off again? Was I fit enough? What if I fell off in the lead and got trampled by the other horses? What would the punters say if I let Dawn and them down again?

An hour before our race, I was so drained of energy with stress that I decided I needed to eat something fast. I was convinced that nothing would do but a banana – not something you find lying around at a racecourse in February. Hils, a true best friend and Cool Dawn supporter, calmly disappeared on a treasure hunt and appeared triumphantly fifteen minutes later with a large bunch of bananas kindly donated by a surprised caterer in the owners' and trainers' bar. I wolfed down a banana and went off to change and weigh out.

Now that Dawn was trained by Robert in his professional year, we were eligible for Robert's stable-sponsorship scheme. All the horses in his yard were sponsored by K.J. Pike and Sons, a local Dorset firm that specialised in repairing and maintaining supermarket trolleys. Jimmy Pike wasn't there to watch me sport his smart red-and-white logo for the first time, but it did make me feel even more like a 'professional' jockey.

Fortunately, it wasn't long before Dawn and I were on our way out of the paddock and down to the start. He didn't show much sign of settling as he towed me towards the starter, and my nerves were running out of control as we lined up at the start. How on earth was I going to keep to my instructions? I think the fan club were also feeling the stresses of our first race since Warwick. As they stood in the stands watching us line up Georgie took a brilliant collection of photos of their worried faces. Thank goodness for all of us that it wasn't long before the race was on.

Dawn didn't leap immediately into the lead as he had at Ascot, but by the time we reached the second fence we were next to the leader Peter Henley on the John Dufosee-trained Sonofagipsy. As soon as we landed Dawn pulled himself into the lead. Much to my surprise he did start to settle then and we were travelling comfortably in front as we jumped the fences in the back straight and turned into the finishing straight for the first time. As we came past the stands we were still going comfortably in the lead, with Teaplanter just behind us in second and the rest of the field stretched out behind us. Proud Sun always made a late run from the back and was settled in there with only a couple of horses behind him. Turning away from home on the second circuit, Dawn thought about running out to the left towards the racecourse stables but within seconds he saw the water jump ahead of him and took hold of the bit again. Teaplanter got closer to us over the next fences, while Proud Sun tripped on landing at the last fence before the back straight and fell. Dawn didn't know that the favourite had fallen and accelerated along the back straight as he felt the other horses get closer and closer. He got close to the fifth last and hit it hard, but the rowing training must have paid off as my legs were still strong and I stayed in the saddle. Rounding the final bend I could feel one horse barely half a length behind. We jumped the third last side by side and I realised it was Teaplanter. Both horses accelerated into and over the second last still neck and neck, while the rest of the field were nowhere in sight. As we approached the last Dawn started to draw clear and I urged him on hoping to see a good stride. We met the fence just right and I really started to kick hard. Dawn changed gear, lengthening his stride and quickly went five lengths clear. He was still accelerating as we passed the winning-post.

It was marvellous, Proud Sun might have fallen but we had beaten a good field with ease. What's more I had managed to stay on even when Dawn made a mistake. We had put Warwick well and truly behind us. As Robert and Andy Miller led us back to the winners' enclosure, I couldn't stop myself from dreaming about our next race. Surely we had earned our place at Cheltenham? The fan club were beaming from ear to ear as I dismounted and carried the great lead weight of my saddle to weigh in. They seemed to think we were Cheltenham-bound.

Although winning a race is always exciting, this was my first real taste of the media circus that would follow us to Cheltenham. John McCririck, the Channel 4 presenter, asked me how much I weighed and I was so overawed by it all that it was four hours later before I realised I should have asked him how much he weighed. Journalists surrounded Robert and he confirmed that we had got the go-ahead – we were going to Cheltenham!

The next morning the racing papers were full of stories of Dawn and me. DAWN OF A NEW ERA was the headline in the *Sporting Life* and the *Racing Post* even said that I 'did nothing wrong'. Surely the closest to actual praise I had ever got while riding. All of the commentators rated Dawn as a very serious contender for the Foxhunters.

There were only three weeks to wait for Cheltenham but it seemed like a year. I went to a business meeting near Cheltenham about ten days before the Festival and drove past the entrance to the racecourse. I had never been to Cheltenham racecourse before and I was sorely tempted to walk the course and be late for the meeting but just driving past had me in a cold sweat of fear. Was I really going to ride in the Foxhunters?

I took the whole of Cheltenham week off work so that I could ride Dawn and make sure I wasn't overtired. There was no way I was going to let myself 'do a Warwick' in the Foxhunters. I watched the TV coverage of the first two days of the Festival with my mother and Georgie Taylor, each day getting more and more nervous. Robert and Sally had a winner on the second day with Flyers Nap, their first winner at Cheltenham, and it simply didn't seem real that in twenty-four hours Dawn and I might be their second. I might have prevented myself from being tired but instead I had all the free time in the world to focus on how nervous I was.

The big day finally arrived and my parents and I set off from Langport for Cheltenham at eight in the morning to make sure that we didn't get stuck in traffic. Our pre-race nerves seemed to have been translated into an absolute obsession about not arriving late. We were so worried about being delayed by traffic that when we stopped to buy the racing papers we decided we didn't even have time for a quick cup of coffee before getting back on the motorway. What we had failed to work out was that only nerve-ridden amateur jockeys and their parents arrive six hours before their race and over four hours before the first race of the day. In retrospect, it's not really surprising that we found very little traffic cluttering the route and arrived in the owners' and trainers' carpark at nine thirty. As our race was at four in the afternoon you could say we were a little early. So early in fact that the course hadn't opened yet and we had to wait for half an hour reading the *Sporting Life* and *Racing Post* in the car because it was too cold to wait outside. Needless to say there were numerous quotes from Terry Selby in the racing papers about my incompetence as a pilot or 'the passenger' as Terry preferred to describe me, all of which did nothing to help steady the nerves.

When the gates opened at ten o'clock, we were the first ones through and into the course. It was pressingly cold and we spent the next couple of hours scouring the trade stands for hats and gloves to keep us warm. I bought a particularly large black felt hat that wasn't very flattering but was the warmest I could find. I never expected that in two years' time it would appear on the front page of the national press.

At noon we met up with John, Alice, Hils and Hugh who had come down together on the train. As well as being Cool Dawn's most important race day ever, 14 March 1996 was also Hils's twenty-ninth birthday and more than a few gin and tonics on the train had helped to calm nerves and celebrate her birthday simultaneously. Hugh and Hils had had baseball caps made with COOL DAWN embroidered into the peak, so the club was official and proud of it. We had arranged to meet the rest of the fan club at Harriet Glen's jewellery stand. Harriet and her husband, David Walsh, were fellow Dorset hunting people and my grandfather had been David's godfather. None of us knew the layout of Cheltenham racecourse very well and it was the only place where we knew we could always leave messages for each other if we got separated. My brother Will and Georgie, with her husband Richard and father Michael, met us there as did several new members of the fan club. James Sanders, an old friend from Oxford and a regular race-goer, and also my parents-in-law who had driven down from Scotland. Most impressively, Mary and Jon King, two friends from Harvard, had come all the way from Minneapolis in the USA. The Cool Dawn fan club had never been so large, so nervous or so cold.

By the time the new arrivals had also kitted themselves out with various hats, gloves and scarves to fend off the freezing temperatures it was time for lunch. Shepherding a group of fifteen people around a busy racecourse is stressful enough even when you're not riding in the biggest race of your life later that day. It was hard work just getting the whole group to congregate in one place and I was getting more and more nervous. John wisely decided that he should take me off on my own to eat something and try to persuade me to calm down. Everyone else went off and had lunch in one of the bars, while John and I went to the owners' and trainers' marquee. He thought this would help me relax but, instead, surrounded by all the famous National Hunt trainers and their owners, I couldn't stop thinking about the race ahead. I forced myself to gulp down each mouthful of a very dry smoked salmon sandwich together with one vodka and lime for Dutch courage and tried hard to persuade my petrified stomach to digest it all. Our race was still three hours away and I needed all the energy I could get.

Robert arrived at the much more sensible time of one o'clock. I left John to keep the fan club under control and met Robert outside the weighing-room. On a normal day's racing there will be a small collection of trainers, officials and jockeys inside the weighing-room. On Gold Cup day an hour before the first race there must have been at least a hundred people filling the weighing-room and the surrounding area beside the paddock. Every racing journalist in the country seemed to be there, as well as countless owners, trainers and jockeys. But if the weighing-room was crowded that was nothing compared to the rest of the racecourse. All of a sudden, Cheltenham seemed to have filled up completely and everywhere I looked there was a sea of people. It took us a good ten minutes just to fight our way towards the rails to walk the course.

Cheltenham is a left-handed course that is about a mile and a half long. There are actually two steeplechase courses – the old and the new. The two courses run parallel to each other with the new on the inside of the old. For the three-day Festival the old course is used for the first two days and the new course is saved until the third day, first for the Cheltenham Gold Cup and then for the Foxhunters. Both races are run over three miles and two furlongs which meant that we would do two and a quarter circuits of the stiff undulating track. We would start at the beginning of the finishing straight and go past the stands, heading gently downhill to the lowest part of the course. Then we would climb to the highest point before turning for home and the steeper downhill run towards the finishing straight. We would do another complete circuit of the course and on the final run up the finishing straight we would continue straight on and run uphill to the finishing-post.

Usually Robert filled me with confidence when we walked the course, but as we approached the first open ditch in the downhill run away from the stands I think even he was having second thoughts. I got to within two yards of the fence when Robert shouted out: 'No need to get any closer, he'll take off from here easily.' The fence looked even larger than Ascot's open ditch and was a great deal taller than me. The second open ditch didn't look any smaller and I started to wonder why on earth I had been so keen to ride at Cheltenham. Robert was also worried about the size of the fences, but thankfully kept his concerns to himself.

We finished walking the course just as the runners in the first race of the day battled their way up the hill towards the finish. Standing by the rails I heard the 'Cheltenham Roar' for the first time – 70,000 punters screaming for their horse all at once. It was a fearsome, loud, growl that raised the hairs on the back of my neck. Would it really be me riding up that hill in a few hours' time? What would all those punters do to me if I messed up like I had at Warwick?

I watched a race or two with the fan club before taking myself off to change. As usual the ladies' changing-room was about a tenth the size of the men's, but whereas usually I found myself the only lady rider of the day changing in a cold, deserted room, on Gold Cup day the ladies' was full to bursting with lady jockeys riding in the Foxhunters, other female amateurs not riding that day, plus friends, family and hangers-on. There was a TV showing the Channel 4 coverage and we all watched the amazing mare Mysilv battle up the hill against Cyborgo in the Stayers Hurdle. The mare had been sixth the previous day in the Champion Hurdle and we all screamed and shouted for such a gallant representative of our gender. Sadly she was beaten by a neck in one the most thrilling finishes of the Festival ever, but it wasn't for lack of vocal support from the lady jockeys.

I didn't watch the next race, the Gold Cup itself, as I was concentrating on changing and weighing out. The race was won by the Irish horse, Imperial Call, and after weighing out I stood on the steps of the weighing-room with all the journalists and watched him with his jockey Conor O'Dwyer receive the reception of a lifetime as they were led back into the winners' enclosure. The Cheltenham winners' enclosure is at one end of the paddock and surrounded on three sides by an amphitheatre of steps. Every spare inch of the steps was filled by a sea of exuberant Irishmen. More jubilant supporters were also flooding into the winners' enclosure behind Imperial Call, all eager to give their horse a pat. It was an extraordinary sight to see on television, let alone from a privileged vantage point ten yards away. The Cheltenham Gold Cup is the highest accolade of steeplechasing and I felt incredibly awestruck to be so close to the winner's celebrations. I had to pinch myself to be sure that I really was standing there all dressed up and ready to ride in the next race. I had always hoped that Dawn and I would be good enough to win a hunter chase but I had never imagined in any wild moment that we would be in with a chance at Cheltenham. Just standing there on the steps watching Imperial Call felt like an achievement beyond all expectations.

The Queen Mother presented Imperial Call's connections with their prizes, the Irish crowd yelled and hollered for all they were worth and I went back to join the other lady amateurs waiting to be called into the paddock. There were seventeen runners in our race of which four were ridden by ladies. Besides me there was Polly Curling riding the Richard Barber-trained What A Hand, Jane Reed (*née* Cobden) on Mr Golightly and Pip Jones on Goolds Gold. What A Hand was joint third favourite at 13–2, just behind Dawn and me at 9–2 and the Irish-trained Elegant Lord at 3–1. Jane and Mr Golightly were at 14–1 while Pip's horse was an outsider at 66–1. Though in the changing-room it didn't matter how the punters rated our chances, we were all scared stiff and at the same time dreaming of what it would feel like to win. I'm sure it wasn't that different in the men's changing-room. The favourite, Elegant Lord, had been third in the Foxhunters the previous year and since then had not been beaten. Enda Bolger, one of the most experienced amateur trainers and jockeys in Ireland, rode him. Enda had won more races than I had ridden in, but he had never won at Cheltenham. I'm sure he was also dreaming of what might be.

I was convinced that Enda and Elegant Lord were our biggest danger, but there were plenty of other good horses in the race. Proud Sun was running and if he could jump the course without falling he was a very real danger. I also fancied Clare Man ridden by Mark Rimmel and Hermes Harvest ridden by Andrew Balding. Both Mark and Andrew were hugely more experienced than me and there was no doubt that they would be able to ride a stronger finish than I could. One of the Irish runners was ridden by Dermot Costello. Dermot's brother, John, had trained Dawn in his Irish point-to-points and John's father-in-law had bred him, so he was almost family. Tim Mitchell and Lewesdon Hill were also in the race. We hadn't raced them since our extra-ordinary victory at the Beaufort, and I was hoping that we wouldn't find the Cheltenham corners as troublesome as the Beaufort's. All in all, it was a strong Foxhunters field and a daunting prospect that Dawn and I were second favourites.

As the minutes ticked by before the race I sat in the changing-room convinced that I didn't have the strength to ride. I was sure I needed more energy so I munched a couple of bananas and several mini Mars Bars, both provided by my mother that morning. This caused much amusement with the other inhabitants of the ladies' changing-room as they were

ABOVE: with my grandfather before my first day's hunting
LEFT: aged three on Ben the donkey
BELOW: Polly and me in a rare moment of togetherness

TOP: Cool Dawn arrives from Ireland looking very skinny

MIDDLE: winning in fine style at Larkhill
(Linda Charles)

LEFT: in the paddock with Andy Miller during Dawn's second season and at his last point-to-point

Wearing the new colours at Kempton (Georgina Taylor)

Looking very small before the race (Georgina Taylor)

ABOVE: where's the mud? Enjoying the well-kept paddock at Kempton
(Georgina Taylor)
RIGHT: weighing in after the race with Harry and Robert
(Georgina Taylor)

ABOVE: regretting eating those Mars Bars before the beginning of the Foxhunters (Georgina Taylor)
LEFT: John and I walk the course at the Irish National (Hugh Harper)
BELOW: the crowd at Cheltenham (Georgina Taylor)

In the lead in the Cheltenham Foxhunters (John Beasley)

Andrew Thornton on his way to winning his first race on Cool Dawn. Here he shows how it should be done (Matthew Webb)

. . . and how it shouldn't (Les Hurley)

convinced I would throw it all up again before the race. And they were very nearly right. Ten minutes later I walked into the paddock feeling distinctly ill. Around the paddock there were people filling every available space, a weight of humanity I could almost feel. The atmosphere was absolutely terrifying and as Robert legged me up on to Dawn I seriously thought I would throw up bananas and Mars Bars all over him. In my point-to-points I had always been afraid of being run away going down to the start, but throwing up on national television, now that was a whole new fear!

I wasn't the only one feeling queasy. My mother was white as a sheet and had been chain-smoking all day with worry. Hugh had recently given up smoking but still smoked an entire pack of Hamlets to try and calm his nerves and cope with the stress of all those about him. Georgie and Hils were in tears because they thought we were about to kill ourselves and John had gone green at the gills with the same thought. As Andy Miller led Dawn and me out on to the track the fan club split up to watch the race on their own. The tension was so high that they all thought Mum might collapse or kill one of them if they said the wrong thing or if the worst happened during the race.

Fortunately, I was unaware of their nerves and before long Dawn and I were cantering down to the start and it started to feel a bit more like a normal race. I still couldn't hold him, and I was still scared of jumping the first fence before the start. We circled for ages because What A Hand had been kicked, but finally we were all called up into a line behind the starting tape. Robert had told me to get on the inside and let Dawn take the lead so I squeezed him in beside Tim Mitchell and Lewesdon Hill about three horses from the inside rail. It seemed as if we waited in the line for an hour, all the time with my banana and mini Mars Bars threatening to make an appearance. Then, all of a sudden, the starter dropped his flag, the tape shot back and we were off.

Dawn took a strong hold as we sped towards the first fence

and we were in the lead by the time we landed. We jumped the next fence in front and I didn't hear or see the crowd as we came past the stands. Behind us Proud Sun had whipped around at the start and was at the back of the field. What A Hand had fallen at the first fence but all the other runners were travelling easily behind us. Still in the lead, we headed out around the top bend and on into the country and then downhill towards the third. This was the fence that Robert thought was the most tricky. It is downhill and you are going deceptively fast into it. We came to it on a long stride and Dawn put in an enormous leap. The horse just behind me, Colonial Kelly, hit the fence hard and I saw his jockey fall to the ground with a thud from the corner of my eye. I didn't really need the reminder that these were big, unforgiving fences.

Suddenly we were approaching the open ditch that Robert wouldn't let me stand beside. I didn't have time to think about how big it was as Dawn accelerated into it and soared over easily. Two more plain fences, and I was still in the lead; and then the next open ditch. Again Dawn was foot perfect, but he was jumping out slightly to the right. This made room for Clare Man and Mark Rimmell and as we reached the top of the hill Clare Man went a length in front of us. As we thundered downhill Dawn really started to pull hard. Robert had said not to let him go too fast towards the downhill fences but there was nothing I could do, Dawn was still too strong for me. He stood back a mile away from the first downhill fence and part of me was convinced that I was going to die there and then. But he sailed over and thundered on towards the next downhill fence. Unlike me he was totally unfazed by the size of his leap.

Clare Man was now on our inside and swerved out across our path into the next fence. Dawn veered to the right as well to avoid him and jumped the fence without mishap. We came past the stands on the outside of the field with Hermes Harvest, Mr Golightly and Clare Man beside us. Dawn jumped the two fences in the finishing straight perfectly and had pulled himself back into the lead. Over what would be the last, Hermes Harvest came up beside us, hit the top of the fence and crashed to the floor. Another reminder of the dangers, but we had survived one circuit of Cheltenham.

Dawn and I headed out on our second circuit still in the lead and I started to think about winning rather than just surviving. We had jumped a whole circuit safely, Dawn was still pulling hard and we certainly had a chance. We jumped the big open ditch a second time. Dawn really made them seem small, and soon we were powering down the hill with only half a mile to go. I could hear the other horses behind me but I had no idea how well they were going. We jumped the downhill fence with ease, but not far behind us Mr Golightly made a mistake and Jane took a nasty fall. Between the third and the fourth last Elegant Lord appeared on my inside. Robert had told me not to push Dawn downhill but to wait until the finishing straight to ride him out so I kept hold of his head as we approached the third-last fence side by side with Elegant Lord. We met the fence wrong and Dawn brushed through the top of it. That was all it took for Elegant Lord to get ahead of us. Enda kicked his horse on and suddenly Elegant Lord was three, four then five lengths clear. I yelled at Dawn, kicked and pushed but we couldn't close the gap. Rationally I knew we were beaten, but I still dared to hope that we might yet catch the leader. Polly Curling was standing beside the last as we jumped it and I heard her screaming, 'Come on, Dido! You can do it!'

I don't remember hearing the rest of the crowd, as all I was thinking about was trying to catch Elegant Lord. Behind us Proud Sun was coming with a late run and Kerry Orchid, another runner, was only a length behind us. But I didn't care about who was behind us, it was who was in front of us that mattered, and all I wanted to do was win. I kicked Dawn on for all I was worth as we galloped up the hill towards the finish but there was nothing we could do. We crossed the finishing line a clear second beaten by a better horse on the day. Seven lengths behind us came Kerry Orchid, who just held on to third from Proud Sun.

My first thoughts were very confused: elated because we had jumped round Cheltenham and had come second; sad because we had been beaten. Some might say I'm never satisfied! My first words to Robert, John and my mother as we arrived in the unsaddling enclosure were, 'I'm sorry we didn't win.' I was terrified that I had let Dawn down again, but gradually it started to occur to me that everyone else in the fan club thought we had done brilliantly. Once Robert had assured me for the tenth time that I hadn't done anything wrong and that we had been beaten by a better horse on the day, I started to relax and accept that we had done something amazing. Dawn had jumped those enormous Cheltenham fences as if they were *cavaletti* and we really had come second.

Together with the fan club, proudly wearing their Cool Dawn caps, I stood in the winners' enclosure and watched Elegant Lord's connections receive the Foxhunters trophy. Enda was a deserving winner and with Imperial Call's victory this second win for Ireland meant that every Irish voice was raised to salute him. Rumour had it that J.P. McManus, the legendary gambler who owned Elegant Lord, had rescued his huge losses from the prior two days of the Festival with their victory. The Christies Foxhunters trophy must be almost four foot high and everyone agreed that although we would have liked to have won, I would have had real trouble picking up the Cup, let alone finding room for it in the car. Next year I would have to come prepared.

After I had weighed in and changed, the whole fan club descended on the owners' and trainers' bar. The bar was full to bursting but we forced our way through to the far corner and I ordered a couple of bottles of Bollinger. Dawn had won over five thousand pounds and I thought the least I could do was buy the drinks. I hadn't figured on the size and exuberance of the fan club because two bottles didn't even give everyone one glass. Two hours later we were exhausted, and I am proud to say that the extended fan club had drunk the bar out of five types of champagne. We may not have won, but our nice, safe, ladies' point-to-pointer had proved that he was one of the top hunter chasers in the country. By the time I left the racecourse I realised that this had been one of the most amazing days of my life.

Two weeks after Cheltenham, Robert called to discuss Dawn's next race. Dawn was still technically a novice for the season and he listed a number of top novice chases as possible options and then said 'or we could try the Irish National'. The Irish Grand National is a top-class stayers handicap worth over one hundred thousand pounds. I didn't really believe Robert meant it to begin with but without really thinking I replied, 'With me riding?' Robert was always a brave man and this occasion was no exception: 'If you want,' came the reply.

If I wanted to ride Dawn in any of the proposed races I needed to get permission from the Jockey Club to ride against professionals. Strictly speaking you have to have had fifteen rides in amateur races or ridden fifteen point-to-point winners to qualify for a licence to ride as an amateur in professional races. I had ridden in five hunter chases and had seven winners in point-to-points so I wasn't quite there. Robert suggested I write to the Jockey Club asking for a permit to be restricted to riding only Dawn against professionals. Not that I had people queuing up to offer me any other rides. He hoped that if I explained that I wanted to keep riding Dawn but at the same time didn't want to limit a good horse's career an exception would be made to the rules. Thankfully the Jockey Club were very understanding and I was duly granted my licence.

Twenty-four hours later we entered Dawn for the Irish National. Whether the Jockey Club would have been so understanding about my permit if they had realised that my first race against professionals would be in the Irish

National, I don't know. But the question remained, did I want to ride him in it?

As I'm writing this now, part of me still wishes that I had decided to ride him, however, in the end, after a lot of heart-wrenching, common sense reigned. There is an enormous difference between amateur racing and the professional game. Dawn and I might have been second in a race at Cheltenham but even I knew that riding against professionals was another league altogether. They ride in up to six races a day, every day, and would have more rides in one week than I would have in a lifetime.

I was determined to prove that I was capable of keeping the ride on Dawn in professional races but starting with the Irish National was a bit silly, even for me. The Irish National was the most valuable steeplechase in the Irish calendar, was live on national TV in the UK and Ireland and there would be no hiding places if I messed up. With a heavy heart I had to admit that it was probably better to have my first race against professionals in a slightly lower-profile event. But as there was very little doubt that Dawn would make the transition from amateur to professional with ease, I was going to have to let him have his first professional race without me.

So it was decided, Dawn would have a crack at the Irish National with a professional jockey. Robert booked Conor O'Dwyer (the Gold Cup hero) to ride him and as soon as that was made public Dawn was made ante-post favourite for the race. Everyone was convinced that he would be much improved by a professional pilot and my phone at Thomas Cook rang constantly with journalists wanting to know how I felt about it. While it was enormously exciting to own the favourite for such a big race, it was also deeply depressing when the reason he was favourite was precisely because I was not riding him. I can't say I was actually looking forward to the race.

The Irish National was run on Easter Monday and to cheer

me up John suggested we spend some of Dawn's Cheltenham winnings and go over to Ireland for a long weekend. Hils and Hugh, never people to miss a good racing party, joined us, and together we flew into Shannon, hired a car and explored some of Cool Dawn's original home country.

Everywhere we went we wore our Cool Dawn baseball caps and proudly told anyone we met that: 'We have a runner in the Irish National.' On the Saturday night we stayed at the Dunraven Arms in Adare which is owned and run by the Murphy brothers. Both brothers were heavily involved in the racing world and Brian Murphy knew Robert well. I have a feeling Robert may have tipped him off about our visit. John and I had only been in our room for ten minutes when the phone ran with reception saying that Mr Murphy thought I might like a quick spin round the local cross-country course and could I be ready in half an hour? I left John contentedly watching the Oxford and Cambridge Boat Race and half an hour later was being legged-up on to an eighteen-hand giant of a horse.

There were six of us, including Brian's brother, and we set off in single file, without any warm-up, at a brisk canter towards an innocuous little post and rails. They were all teasing me for riding too short like a jockey and I was more than a little suspicious that they would be trying to make a fool out of me. Nonetheless, the giant jumped nicely enough and wasn't in the least concerned as we galloped towards the next fence, which was a four-foot stone wall. I was just starting to relax and think that the horse seemed safe enough when one of the group yelled out: 'Hurry up Dido, that horse went round Badminton a few years ago, what are you going so slowly for?' We spent the next hour roaring round the cross-country course over huge drops, in and out of water and over some big, solid-looking walls. I might have jumped Cheltenham fences but at least all those fences were the same. I was extremely glad to be riding such a well-balanced and obedient horse who appeared to know what to expect around every corner. Dawn may have more power and scope but his flat-out gallop approach to jumping any and all obstacles would have landed us in some serious trouble.

Needless to say, wherever we went we found Irishmen with horses to sell us. John was starting to get seriously worried that I might give in and buy one so he replied to every offer of a horse by saying he had one to sell too. 'Cool Dawn – but the starting price is one hundred thousand pounds!' He thought it was terribly funny but I was very worried that someone might not realise he was joking. At least I hoped he was joking.

On the Sunday evening Hils, Hugh, John and I met Robert in Dublin for supper. Irish Distillers, who were sponsoring the race, had provided a charter plane free of charge. Robert and Andy had flown over with Dawn and the other two English runners Jodami and Norman Conqueror. It was the first time one of Robert's horses had ever travelled in a plane and we were very definitely the country yokels in the world of big-time racing.

In fact, Dawn wasn't the first member of his family to compete in the Irish National even if it was the first time for all his human connections. Although his dam, Aran Tour, never raced, his granddam, Frantouri, was third in the Irish National in 1978 and, incredibly, won a two-mile chase the following day. On the other side of his pedigree four sons of Dawn's remarkable sire, Over The River, had been placed in Irish nationals: Cool Ground, Zeta's Lad, River Tarquin and Over The Road. So Dawn was following in a good family tradition.

Our first experience of Irish racing could not have been more different from Cheltenham. At Cheltenham there are lots of separate carparks for VIPs, owners, trainers, jockeys etc., and if you don't have the right car sticker you don't get in. At Fairyhouse it was somewhat easier. We simply drove to the main gates, leant out of the car window and said the magic words: 'We've got a runner in the National.' Then drove into a space right beside the ticket stiles.

I was so accustomed to walking the course because I was riding, that it didn't feel like racing not to. So I insisted that Hils, Hugh, John and I walked the course before lunch. In theory, only owners, trainers and jockeys were allowed on to the course and I'm not sure that the man on the gate believed that the short blonde girl in front of him could possibly be the owner of a runner. But we all put our Cool Dawn baseball caps on and that seemed to convince him.

The Irish National is run over three miles and five furlongs, much the longest trip that Dawn had ever tried. Unlike the Aintree Grand National, the fences were just the same as any other steeplechase. The course was right handed, with long flat straights and the horses would do two circuits of the course. The ground was on the firm side, but Dawn had won at Ascot on similar ground so we were hopeful it would suit him. Part of me still believed that I would be riding as we walked from fence to fence, but as the course had no inside running rail, another part of me was relieved that it wouldn't be my fault if Dawn ran out this time.

After walking the course we met up with the rest of the official fan club for lunch. My aunt, who lives in Ireland and who had been faithfully watching all Dawn's hunter chases in her local bookies, joined us for the first time, and Cool Dawn's Cheltenham prize money also paid for my parents and younger brother to fly out from Heathrow for the day. It wasn't just Robert and Cool Dawn who felt they were joining the racing jet-set.

Irish Distillers laid on a superb lunch including liberal quantities of Irish whiskey. I was starting to see why people enjoy owning racehorses without riding them. Halfway through lunch Tim Thomson-Jones said that Tracy Piggott was looking for me and she wanted to interview me for Irish television. I left everyone eating pudding to go and do my first live TV interview, confident that it couldn't be too embarrassing because all my nearest and dearest were nowhere near a TV. Unfortunately, I couldn't have been more wrong. As Tracy

Piggott was asking me what advice I'd give Conor O'Dwyer, someone managed to find a TV for the sponsor's lunch tent and I'm reliably informed that the whole of the sponsor's lunch tent stopped eating to laugh at my attempts not to look upset at losing the ride. When I walked back into the tent ten minutes later everyone gave me a round of applause and the only reason I did not go bright red with embarrassment was because I was already blushing from the interview itself.

Before I knew it, it was time to prepare for the race. It felt very strange helping Robert saddle Dawn and than standing in the paddock listening to him give Conor his instructions. There were twenty runners in the race and the paddock was crammed full of connections admiring their horses, but somehow I doubt that any of the other owners were secretly wishing that they were riding. Dawn looked superb and I couldn't help feeling enormously proud of him even if it did feel that this time Cinderella wasn't going to the ball.

Although Dawn had started the day ante-post favourite by the time the Irish punters had placed their bets on the racecourse he had been pushed back to fifth in the betting. The favourite was Jodami, another of the English runners, at 5–1. Jodami had won the Cheltenham Gold Cup a couple of years before and was carrying eleven stone twelve pounds compared to Dawn's ten stone. Next in the betting came three Irish horses, all with decent handicap form – Go Go Gallant, Fissure Seal and Lord Singapore. They were all at 7–1, with Dawn next in the betting at 15–2. It looked a wide-open race with another two horses at 8–1, Son of War and Feathered Gale, and several others at longer than 15–1.

We crammed into the owners' and trainers' stand and suddenly it hit me, my precious horse was about to race without me. It is not unheard of for steeplechasers to be killed racing. What would I do if Dawn was badly injured? When I was riding, I was so busy worrying about being hurt myself that I couldn't have time to worry about Dawn as well. Now I wasn't riding I was terrified that Dawn would be hurt. I'm rather ashamed to say that I didn't worry about Conor, rather what I would do to Conor if he hurt Dawn!

As the starter dropped his flag and they set off towards the first fence I could hardly watch. I stood either side of Hils and my mother, one step higher than them in the stands, with a hand on each of their shoulders. Dawn set off towards the fence at top speed and was in the lead by the time he landed over it. By the second Dawn had a couple of lengths lead and I had started to grip Hils and Mum's arms with all my strength. Over each jump I was convinced that Dawn would hurt himself and it seemed a complete miracle that he cleared the fences easily.

Dawn led the field for the whole of the first circuit and had all the other horses stretched out behind him as he set a fast pace. By the time the runners came past the stands he was still jumping smoothly some five lengths in the lead. Going out into the country again he made two bad mistakes when Conor tried to drive him into the fences. Dawn just wasn't used to being told what to do and refused to listen to Conor's instructions. I was finding it hard to cope with the stress of watching and I had nearly cut off the circulation in Mum's and Hils's arms. Dawn briefly lost the lead to Go Go Gallant and then jumped back in front as the leaders rounded the final bend with four fences still to go. I felt completely sick with fear and excitement. We all screamed for Cool, then Hils and Mum screamed for me to let go of their arms before their circulation stopped! For one second Dawn looked as if he might win, but as he approached the last fence Jodami and Feathered Gale were up beside him both looking ominously full of running. As Dawn landed over the last, the other two horses surged past him and he crossed the line in third place with Jodami second and Feathered Gale the winner.

Dawn looked completely exhausted as Andy led him back into the unsaddling enclosure, but not as exhausted as I was. I was utterly drained with the emotion and worry of watching him. I had expected to resent not riding him, but instead I just found it too scary. When I rode Dawn, I might have been scared stiff up until the start of the race, but once the race was underway, I was always concentrating too hard to worry too much about the dangers. Watching Dawn, I found I had far too much time to worry about what might go wrong and it was certainly not an experience I wanted to repeat. For the first time I realised what hell it must be for John and my parents to watch me race.

Having said all that, I was enormously proud of Dawn. Coming third certainly justified bringing him to Ireland and it was fabulous publicity for Robert so early in his professional training career. As Andy led Dawn away to the racecourse stables, Robert asked me what the third prize money was. I hadn't even thought to look and we were all amazed when we realised Dawn had won nine thousand pounds. We had tried hard to spend the Cheltenham winnings on our luxury tour of Ireland, but in fact we would be going back having made a small fortune. Maybe there was some compensation for giving up the ride!

As the 1996 season came to a close it was increasingly clear that Dawn was a superbly talented horse. When Mackenzie and Selby published their long-awaited annual review of point-to-pointers and hunter chasers they didn't beat about the bush: 'Would be perfect for a chase like the Hennessy, but the sky's the limit.' For the first year ever, I also came in for some praise, with Terry Selby saying that I had 'actually got him jumping better than Gold Cup hero, Conor O'Dwyer'. It was fantastic to get my first ever good 'school report', and it almost made up for not riding him. Almost, but not quite. As the autumn approached there was only one thing I was certain about. Although the Irish National had been a fantastic experience, I was determined to get the ride back next season.

Chapter Five

The Wilderness Year

As the start of the 1996–97 National Hunt season approached I was feeling very confident. Robert and I had decided that Dawn should turn professional full time and run in handicaps in the autumn. To my great delight Robert had also agreed that I could ride him. We would find a nice, low-profile handicap for me to have my first race against professionals and then, with any luck, Dawn and I would progress to some of the top staying handicaps of the season.

Every season Dawn had moved effortlessly up a grade and I was starting to take it for granted that he would do exactly the same again. As I puffed away on the rowing machine, I dreamed of winning the Hennessy on him and maybe even riding in the Irish National myself the following spring. But racehorses are a great leveller and pride invariably comes before a fall.

I was just about to get into my boss's car to drive to a meeting at Heathrow on 27 August 1997, when my secretary, Fee, ran out to the carpark in Peterborough to say that Sally Alner was on the phone and needed to speak to me urgently. I went back to my desk wondering what could be urgent at this time of year. Dawn had been in work for a couple of months but he was at least six weeks away from his first race and there weren't any entries to do or decisions to take for at least a month. As soon as I heard Sally's voice I knew something was wrong and she didn't beat around the bush. Dawn had been run over by a tractor. He was badly cut on all four legs, though, thank God he hadn't broken any bones. Fortunately, Sarah, the girl riding him, wasn't hurt either, though she was extremely shaken.

The string had been out on exercise that morning walking along the narrow lanes of Dorset, as they did most days. A large tractor had approached the string at a fair speed scaring some of the younger horses. The horse in front of Dawn had rooted himself to the spot while the one behind him panicked and pushed Dawn into the middle of the road right into the path of the oncoming tractor. Dawn had been knocked to the ground and by the time the tractor came to a halt one of its wheels was resting on top of Dawn's legs.

Somehow Dawn was alive, but only because he had remained so calm. Plenty of horses would have struggled and panicked but he just lay there until the tractor had reversed off him. Everyone had assumed that once he got up from the ground they would be able to see that at least one of his legs was limp and broken. But although there was plenty of blood pouring down his legs, he heaved himself up and stood steadily on all four feet, with no obvious breaks. As a safety precaution, he was wearing knee-pads, which had been ripped to shreds. If he hadn't been wearing them he would surely have been much more seriously injured.

While Kathy, the head girl, went to call Locketts for help, the rest of the lads (mostly girls) used their T-shirts as impromptu bandages to try and stem the bleeding on Dawn's legs. Robert drove one of the lorries out immediately, expecting to have to call out the local vet to shoot one of his horses. It was only once he got past the crowd of semi-hysterical topless girls that surrounded Dawn that he realised that it was his stable star that was injured. Thankfully, the humane killer wasn't necessary and to everyone's amazement Dawn managed to walk into the lorry unaided. Once they got him back to the yard, he quietly walked into his stable and calmly started eating his hay.

I simply couldn't believe it. Fee tells me that I went white as a sheet, but I couldn't ask too many questions because my boss was waiting for me. He had been expecting to have a business discussion with me as we drove down to Heathrow from Peterborough. Instead he drove while I made a series of increasingly distressed phone calls to the Cool Dawn fan club.

If I could have done, I would have dropped everything and driven to Dorset immediately. But while my boss was understanding about his journey being disrupted, he didn't have time for a detour to Dorset to visit an equine car-crash victim. Instead, I called my parents and asked them to go and visit Dawn as soon as they could. Then I called Hils.

As well as being a core member of the fan club, Hils is also a solicitor who specialises in litigation and does a substantial amount of work in horse-racing and related equine fields. After she had recovered from the incredible shock and I had reassured her that Dawn was going to be fine, her legal brain sprang into gear. She ensured that I had a note of what happened in detail and asked whether the driver might have been at fault. Unfortunately, I didn't have Dawn insured, but she thought that if the driver had been at fault his vehicle insurance might well cover any losses I incurred, just as if Dawn had been a car. If Dawn was seriously harmed then maybe I could get some compensation. Especially, she said, if the worst happened and his injuries turned out to be fatal. Fatal? Dawn couldn't die. Unthinkable. I could not focus on her legal advice because I simply couldn't cope with the thought that Dawn might be permanently injured or worse.

That afternoon Brian Eagles, Robert's vet, came to visit Dawn. By then, he was very lame and sore. He had nasty cuts on all four legs but thankfully it didn't look as if any tendons or bones were damaged. All four legs were swollen and swathed in bandages but fortunately no long-term damage had been done. Nonetheless, it would be several weeks before Dawn could go back into work and it would be a while before he would be able to race again, if ever. It was a very real lesson that racing is not just a sport of fairytales. From the peak of the Foxhunters and the Irish National we had fallen to the bleak prospect of maybe never race-riding together again.

Dawn was confined to his stable for three weeks and recovered incredibly fast. He even made it back into full work by the beginning of October. Thankfully, he seemed unperturbed by his accident. We were all very concerned that he would have become terrified of traffic, but we needn't have worried; fear is not an emotion Dawn is very familiar with. Robert rode him himself on his first day back on the roads just in case he was afraid of the traffic but apart from tensing up just a little when a large tractor came past him, Dawn was completely calm. He has never shown any fear of traffic since.

By the end of October Dawn seemed well and he was nearly ready for his first race. John and I were due to go to New Zealand for a wedding in the middle of November and I was very keen to get one race on Dawn before we went away. In retrospect, Dawn could probably have done with a week's more work before his first run but I made the mistake of putting my social diary ahead of his best interests. It was a very costly mistake.

On Saturday, 9 November, Dawn had his first race of the 1996–97 season at Sandown and I had my first race against professionals. The build-up before the race was as terrifying as ever. After the media hype of the Foxhunters and the Irish National I was becoming more accustomed to talking to racing journalists. On the Friday afternoon I had a call from a journalist from *The Sun* who wanted to run a story about a lady amateur riding her own horse. When he heard that Saturday was also my birthday he knew he had a story. In *The Sun* the next day, they described me as 'the gorgeous Dido' which made John quite upset until I pointed out I'd never met the author and only spoken to him on the phone. Men can be so sensitive!

I was incredibly nervous about riding against professionals. Everybody had told me that there was a quantum difference in ability between even very good amateurs (which I wasn't) and the true pros. Others had warned me that they might try to interfere with me and psych me out. Not that they needed to, I was nervous enough to be useless anyway.

Robert had runners elsewhere that day, so Sally came to Sandown to look after Dawn and me together with the ever-faithful Andy Miller. Sally and I walked the course and I think both of us got increasingly nervous with every stride. The course is right-handed and set on the side of a hill. Dawn's race was over three miles, that meant we would start going downhill away from the stands. We would jump one fence and then turn sharply right into the long, back straight with seven fences all in a row. The Waterloo to Exeter train line runs parallel to the back straight. Dad had ridden at Sandown years before and whenever we had gone to London on the train as a family I had listened to his tales of riding there and mused on the unlikely event of my doing the same one day. The last three fences in the back straight are called the railway fences because they are directly beside the railway line. As Sally and I approached them, it occurred to me that today all those musings were becoming a bit too close to reality for comfort! The railway fences are infamous, they come three in a row in quick succession and many a good horse and rider have been found out there. Suddenly my childhood fantasies didn't seem so sensible after all. It was a long walk round the right-hand bend at the end of the straight and up the hill to the finish and with every step I was wondering quite how smart it was trying to fulfil childhood fantasies in real life. Not very smart at all was what my gut was saying to me.

Once we had walked the course, I took myself off to change and eat the ritual banana and it wasn't long before I was being called into the paddock to greet the fan club. Only a select few had been able to make it to Ireland and it was nice to see a full complement back to support us. In addition to Mum and Dad and Hils and Hugh, Georgie and her father had driven up from Dorset, James Sanders had come from London, as had Alice and a friend of hers who was staying for the weekend. There was no doubt that after Ascot, Alice was becoming increasingly addicted to this racing lark. As it was my birthday even my brother Will had come to watch as well.

I walked into the paddock with the four professional jockeys also riding in the race. Much to my surprise, far from psyching me out, the professionals greeted me warmly with broad grins. Conor O'Dwyer was one of them and he was keen to find out how his Irish National mount had fared during the summer. I don't think he believed me when I said he had been run over by a tractor! Conor was riding Betty's Boy, a seven-year-old horse who had won two of his four novice chases the previous season. He had been placed in the championship novice chase at Cheltenham but his handicap rating meant that he carried ten pounds less weight than Dawn. Another friendly face was Chris Maude riding Inchcailloch. Chris was West-Country based and I had ridden against his half-brother, Rupert Nuttall, many times in local point-to-points. Inchcailloch had won the Tote Cesarewitch on the flat on his last outing and there was no doubt that he stayed and would be fit and another very serious contender. The other two runners and riders were Grey Smoke ridden by Jason Titley and Willsford ridden by Gerry Hogan. They too greeted me with smiles and I tried to relax and return the greeting.

The professionals may have been friendly in the paddock, but by the time we were circling at the start they all became very serious. There was none of the nervous chit-chat of a point-to-point and it was clear from their attitude that they meant business. They quizzed me about my riding plans but somehow managed not to answer my questions about their own. Dawn and I lined up behind the starting tape and I felt like an absolute novice and totally and completely out of my depth. Strangely they had suceeded in psyching me out in the most subtle manner!

The tape was down and before I knew it we were hurtling towards the first fence. Dawn jumped the fence well just behind Willsford and Grey Smoke, then hurtled on towards the sharp right-hand bend. Dawn and I have never been very good with corners and this was to be no exception. He was pulling hard and we went very wide round the outside. I knew he jumped to the right and I really did not want to be on the outside so as soon as I could I pulled him inside the other horses. We had Grey Smoke and Willsford on our left with Inchcailloch and Betty's Boy tucked in behind us.

The next fence was upon us, but something odd happened. Dawn suddenly wasn't jumping like his usual self. Normally he would accelerate into each fence of his own accord, but this time he didn't seem to want to jump. He slowed down into the second, losing valuable ground and jumped high and slow over it. As soon as he landed he grabbed hold of the bit and towed us into the lead. I had never known him like this and really didn't know what to do. At the next, the open ditch, again he decelerated and again we made a real meal of the fence losing a couple of lengths. At the water he jumped badly right interfering with the second horse, Grey Smoke. Jason Titley cursed me with an 'effing amateurs' thrown in for good measure. This was not turning out to be much fun.

Suddenly the railway fences were upon us, but I wasn't thinking about them at all, I was concentrating on trying to keep Dawn straight. There are no running rails on the inside along the back straight at Sandown and I was terrified that Dawn would run out. Despite jumping slightly to the right Dawn showed no sign of running out this time. Before I knew it we had jumped the railway fences in slightly better style than the previous fences and were turning towards the stands still in the lead.

For the next mile things seemed slightly more under control. Dawn remained in the lead with Grey Smoke tracking us and the other three horses a couple of lengths behind. As we approached the railway fences the second time, I did have time to recall daydreaming about jumping these fences as a child. Maybe riding against professionals wasn't that bad after all. We met the three railway fences right but as we landed over the last railway fence and started into the long turn for home Grey Smoke nipped past us going at some speed. Once again Dawn and I were very unbalanced round the corner and we lost several lengths going into the third last. We met it wrong and Dawn put in a short stride. Inchcailloch and Betty's Boy came past us and we were now labouring in fourth. Our earlier jumping mistakes had taken a lot of energy out of him and he was getting very tired. We clambered over the last two fences and in the run in I asked him for a final effort to see if we could catch the third, Conor O'Dwyer and Betty's Boy. Dawn bravely stretched out as best he could, but it was not enough and we finished a very tired fourth with only Willsford behind us.

Andy led us back to the unsaddling enclosure and I weighed in with mixed feelings. As usual after a race, the sheer fact that I had taken it on and survived was exhilarating, but I knew that I had not put up the best riding performance of my life. In fact I had given Dawn no help at all and I knew that we should have been better than fourth. If only I had been able to get him jumping better to begin with. I could tell that Sally and the fan club agreed with my self-criticism from the glum looks on their faces. If I were to continue riding Dawn against professionals I would have to do a lot better than that. But worse was yet to come.

Two days later, I called Robert to check that Dawn was well and to discuss entries for the next couple of months. But all was not well at all. That morning Robert had found some heat and swelling in Dawn's off foreleg. Brian Eagles had been called and the diagnosis was not good. Dawn had damaged a ligament and needed three months of box rest at the very least. We wouldn't be making any more entries for some time.

I still don't know for certain what caused Dawn's injury but there is no doubt that both his car crash and my insistence on running before going to New Zealand certainly aggravated it. His off fore was the least badly cut of all four legs in August and so would have borne most of his weight in the first week or two of his recovery. Equally by running him when he wasn't a hundred per cent fit, we had again put the leg under more strain than was necessary. All in all, there was ample scope for me to blame myself, and I did.

Dawn spent the next three months confined to his box while the rest of us prayed that he would eventually recover. There was no way of knowing for sure how long it would take or whether he would ever be back to full strength but we certainly wouldn't be racing in the near future, and not until next season at the earliest.

By January, the heat and swelling in Dawn's leg had gone down and Robert and Brian decided to fire both his front legs. This is a fairly gruesome procedure that involves burning the skin and tendon sheath in the lower leg with a red-hot poker. The intention is that they will tighten and thicken and therefore provide more support to the damaged leg. Obviously, Dawn was under local anaesthetic during the operation, but it was still fairly horrific to think of his lovely clean legs being scarred for life. The operation seemed to have gone well but it was too early to tell whether his leg would stand the stress of training and racing again.

It was about this time that I was reminded of my legal advice following the tractor incident. If we could establish that the accident had caused Dawn's injury then I might be reimbursed for my vet fees, training fees and lost income from prize money. I had to accept the possibility that Dawn might never see a racecourse again and that I would need all the money I could get to save up for another horse. Robert and Brian were not able to be completely certain that the car crash was the root cause of Dawn's injury, but they were sure that at the very least it had made his leg more susceptible to damage. Hils felt that this was enough to start discussions with the insurance company involved and she set about gathering evidence together.

Unfortunately, not all the evidence was in our favour. Hils got copies of all the statements the lads had made about the accidents and they were, to say the least, a bit contradictory. The statements had been taken by a local policeman two weeks after the incident so it's probably not surprising that everyone's memories differed. But, unfortunately, they differed quite a lot. One said the tractor was going at forty miles an hour while another thought it was nearer fifteen miles per hour. All, however, were united in believing that the vehicle had been going dangerously fast down a narrow lane towards the group of horses. This was enough for Hils to get a serious response from the other side's insurance company and she felt confident that she could get me at least some of my costs back.

In the middle of April, however, Hils got some more slightly startling evidence; the manufacturers of the tractor stated that when fully loaded – as the tractor had been that day – it has a maximum speed of five miles per hour. So whatever else it was doing, it couldn't have been careering down the lane at fifteen miles per hour, let alone forty! I still do not know exactly how she did it, but despite this crucial fact, Hils managed to persuade the loss adjuster handling the case that the driver was at fault and I duly received a payment of seven thousand pounds. If Dawn could never race again, at least I could now afford to buy another horse and we could start all over again.

After another six weeks in his box to recover from the operation, Dawn was turned out in a field to convalesce and all I could do was hope that he would be all right for next season. For the previous three years the spring had been a time for the worry, excitement and exhilaration of racing. With no racing to look forward to, the spring of 1997 was going to be very grey and boring in comparison. Little did I know how grey.

While I had been enjoying my race-riding, John had been working away at his own hobby, politics. He had always wanted to become a Member of Parliament and had been selected to represent the Conservatives in the 1997 election. John's constituency was a very safe Labour seat in west London called Ealing Southall, so we weren't exactly packing our bags and expecting to be in Westminster by May! Nonetheless, in April, John was on a leave of absence from his paid job and working eighteen hours a day on his campaign.

As I had discovered at the Irish National, I am not a natural spectator, and I can't say I found it very easy to follow behind John, kissing babies and playing the adoring Tory wife. But fortunately racing even managed to work its way into his campaign.

On the last Saturday before the election John and I were handing out leaflets on Southall Broadway. Southall is one of the strongest centres of Asian culture in Europe. Instead of the usual British high street shops, Southall Broadway has a fabulous collection of foreign supermarkets, imported sari shops and Indian restaurants. It's not traditional Tory country and it promised to be a difficult afternoon. As it happens, the last Saturday in April is also the day of the Whitbread Gold Cup and I had willingly agreed to come out and help the consituency workers because John had assured me that I could stop off in a bookies to watch the race. Robert had three runners, one of which, Harwell Lad, was ridden by fellow amateur Rupert Nuttall, and I was keen to support them as best I could, even from a distance.

At about three o'clock I left John and his team visiting a local supermarket and went to find a bookies. Unsurprisingly, in Southall horse-racing had a much more universal and compelling appeal than the Conservative Party and there was a Tote betting shop crammed full of people about a hundred yards down the road. When I walked in I took off my blue rosette so as not to appear too conspicuous but I might as well not have bothered. I was the only woman and the only non-Asian in the shop. While I stood by the screen watching the runners circle at the start I could feel everyone's eyes on me. One of the locals asked me whom I had backed. 'No one,' I replied, 'I never bet.' This raised a murmur of curiosity in the shop and it wasn't long before everyone there knew about Cool Dawn and Locketts and my passion for racing.

They all wanted to know which of Robert's three horses had the best chance. The three runners were Bishop's Hall, Flyer's Nap and Harwell Lad. I didn't know much about Bishop's Hall, but I really fancied Flyer's Nap, who had won for Robert at Cheltenham the previous year. Harwell Lad was another thing altogether. He had arrived from Ireland at the same time as Dawn and had been completely unrideable. Harry Wellstead had bought him from Tom Costello but I don't think either of them expected great things from him. In the yard we all called him 'Junior' and Junior was infamous. He was the cleverest and most talented horse I had ever seen but he was also totally unpredictable. He did everything by his rules and his rules only. In his first point-to-point his jockey, Tim Mitchell, kicked him in the ribs at the start and Junior simply bucked him off and stood stock still while the rest of the field galloped away towards the first fence. Rupert Nuttall rode him because he was about the only jockey who seemed to be able to coax him into racing. Junior was never a horse to risk your money with and the Whitbread was no exception. Luckily for them, the punters of Southall took no notice of my advice.

Everyone (except me!) just had time to put a quick bet on Junior and Flyer's Nap and the race was on. After the first circuit Flyer's Nap looked to be going very well and I began to think he might win. As they came towards the third last, Flyer's Nap was out in front and we were all yelling for him but Harwell Lad and Rupert were nowhere in sight. Suddenly something clicked in Junior's brain and he and Rupert went into overdrive. They went into second as they approached the pond fence and then drew clear of the field. I could hardly believe my eyes. The Southall Tote was in uproar with everyone screaming for Rupert and Junior. They cleared the last safely several lengths in front and crossed the line comfortably in the lead with Flyer's Nap a good second. None of us could believe it. I was so pleased for Robert, Sally, Rupert and Harry – what an achievement to win the Whitbread. The Southall Tote erupted and it finally dawned on me that the whole shop had had a dual forecast on Junior and Flyer's Nap. As they all collected their money someone asked me when I would be coming back – with another tip for them. In a moment of madness, I whipped out my blue rosette and shouted across the room, 'Only if you all vote Conservative and vote for my husband!'

John and I spent the next week pacing the streets of Ealing Southall and I didn't think anything more of my visit to the bookies until election day. On election day itself it is traditional for the candidate and his spouse to visit all the polling stations during the day and as John and I toured the Southall polling stations that afternoon it seemed as if word had got round about the Whitbread. The Labour activists at every polling booth repeatedly ignored John but greeted me with open arms and requests for more tips. I probably didn't help John get any more votes, but the Cool Dawn fan club had just acquired a few more members!

Predictably, John lost his election; 1997 just did not seem to be our year.

Chapter Six

Losing the Ride and
Learning to be an Owner

By the summer of 1997 John and I had recovered from the exhaustion of the election and it looked like Dawn's leg was completely healed. He went back into work at Locketts in the middle of July and I dared to start thinking once more of racing glory. As I rowed away in our London flat, watching my videos of Cheltenham, I dreamt of riding Dawn against the professionals, of winning a handicap on him and maybe of riding in one of the handicaps at Cheltenham. All far beyond my early expectations of Dawn or my riding career.

By the middle of August Dawn was ready to start fast work and I was determined to be in the saddle when he had his first gallop. Robert and Sally's gallops are in one of the most beautiful parts of the West Country on the edge of the Dorset downs. From the top you can see across the Blackmore Vale to Stourhead, and on a very clear day you can see the Mendips some fifty miles away in the distance. The gallops themselves are a tough three-furlong climb straight up the side of the hill on old downland turf. Dawn was always keen at the beginning of the season and despite his long holiday this year was no exception. He bucked and kicked as we walked down the hill with four other horses to start our first piece of work. He was really excited and caught me totally by surprise when he whipped around at the bottom of the hill. Half a second later I was lying on the ground watching his hindquarters disappear up the hill. It was a long walk up and I was puffing pretty hard as the rest of the string galloped past me. When I finally got to the top, completely out of breath, I found Robert holding Dawn, both of them laughing at me in their own way. It was a very embarrassing experience.

Unfortunately, worse was to come. Two weeks later Dawn did exactly the same thing to me on the gallops. Humiliation. Then the next day we were cantering along the flat in one of Robert's large fields with the rest of the string watching us when Dawn completely ran away with me. I could tell that Robert, as polite and reserved as ever, was beginning to lose patience with me. I was riding the best horse in his yard and I couldn't even stay under control on the flat. Heaven knows what would happen when we started jumping. When I went down to Dorset the next weekend, Robert took me aside and suggested that he arrange some lessons for me before Dawn's first race. He said he was keen that I 'didn't have another disaster like Sandown' and he made it clear that I needed to improve considerably to carry on riding against professionals. For the first time, I started to wonder if I might have to give up the ride if Dawn was to fulfil his potential. It was a very un-pleasant thought and I came back to London deeply depressed.

Robert arranged for Dawn and me to go to Yogi Breisner for lessons. Yogi is one of the UK's, if not the world's, best horse and jockey trainers. Many of the best jump-jockeys and event riders have been coached by him, and if he couldn't help me no one could. The plan was for me to take a week off work and to stay with Yogi at his base in Oxfordshire. Yogi said he had seen my performance at Sandown and viewed training me as 'a big challenge', so I was under no illusions about his opinion of me.

Dawn and I arrived at Waterstock, near Thame in

Oxfordshire, at the beginning of October for what was to prove to be one of the most exhausting weeks of my life. Every morning and most afternoons I jumped Dawn in the indoor school under Yogi's watchful eye and on most days I rode a couple of other horses in between as well. 'You are nowhere near fit enough,' was Yogi's straightforward assessment after I had turned red, then purple, then green during our first hour-long session. He was right. By the third day, I was so tired that I went to bed at seven o'clock in the evening as soon as I had fed Dawn his supper.

As well as being tiring, my week with Yogi was enormously educational. Yogi is one of those very rare top-flight horsemen who can communicate not just with horses but with human beings as well. By the middle of the week he had made me realise that virtually everything I did instinctively on a horse was wrong. I leant back when you should lean forward, kicked when you should sit still and braked when you should accelerate. I had to learn to race-ride virtually from scratch.

First Yogi made me change the whole way I sat on a horse. In the pony club I was always taught to keep my heels down with only my toes in the stirrups. Yogi wanted me to put the stirrups as far back towards my heels as possible and keep my toes down and bent in towards the horse. Apparently I tensed my knees when I was meant to relax them and arched my back when I was meant to keep it straight. It was a lot to think about before we even got as far as jumping a fence.

Once I had mastered this strange new way of sitting in the saddle we moved on to jumping. Every day, Yogi would set up one small jump in the indoor school and Dawn and I would canter round and round jumping it straight out of his stride. Yogi's theory was that unlike show-jumping you shouldn't try and see a stride but just get lower and lower in the saddle as the horse approached the fence and let him find his own stride. The key was good forward impulsion from at least six or seven strides away, rather than checking and riding the horse for a specific stride. What I wouldn't have given to have been taught that ten years earlier! Every day I fell off at least once, but as each lesson went by I felt more and more in control. On our last day Yogi let me school Dawn outside over some larger fences in an enormous field. Although I fell off twice as usual, Dawn jumped well and Yogi assured me that I was much improved. There was no doubt about that, but my concern was whether I had improved enough.

The next week, I went down to Dorset to show Robert what I had learnt. Robert wanted to see me jump Dawn to prove that I was up to riding him in his first race. As usual Dawn got thoroughly over-excited once he realised that he was going to jump and whipped around and bucked as we trotted to the bottom of the schooling field. I didn't fall off and thought to myself that at least I had passed the first part of the test. Dawn and I jumped seven or eight fences with Robert and the rest of the string watching. It was a while since Dawn had jumped steeplechase fences and he wasn't accelerating into his fences as much as Robert would have liked but he agreed with Yogi's assessment of me. I had improved enough to be allowed to keep the ride, for the time being.

Our first big test was to be at Wincanton on 8 November in the Badger Beer Chase. It was almost exactly a year since my last ride in a race. John and I drove down to Wincanton in the morning and I was green with fear by the time we reached the course. I am always very nervous before the first race of the season but this was much the worst ever. It had been a long time since my last race at Sandown and I knew that that had been a disaster. Although Yogi had taught me an enormous amount, he had also, in a strange way, shattered my confidence. I had never before really known how bad a jockey I was. Somehow, now that I knew how incompetent I had been, I was much more nervous about my ability to succeed, even though I also knew that I had improved beyond all recognition. With a couple of hours to go before the race I wasn't thinking very rationally at all.

As soon as we arrived, I met Robert to walk the course and get my instructions. The ground was perfect and the fences looked quite manageable compared to Cheltenham, but I was still petrified of failing.

The Wincanton course is a fairly flat right-handed course. There are three fences in the long run past the stands, followed by a gentle right-hand turn towards the water jump. Another gentle turn takes you into the back straight and four fences all in a line. Then you turn right again towards the only downhill fence and on from there back into the finishing straight again. As we walked into the back straight Robert pointed out the two-and-a-half-mile start. This would have been helpful, if it weren't that we were entered in a three-mile race. Robert thought the Badger Beer was a two-and-a-half-mile race and when I corrected him he looked concerned. As we walked round the bend in the finishing straight he started to explain that if we were in the lead, this is where we would be challenged. When he said that I shouldn't worry if Dawn was overtaken here I knew he wasn't expecting us to win. He had one other surprise for me, he didn't want Dawn and me to make the running. He felt that at this level you couldn't win races from the front and that Dawn needed to learn to settle in behind and take the lead only towards the end of the race. So our instructions were to jump off in the middle of the field. This added a whole new fear: how on earth was I going to hold Dawn back?

I took myself off to change and before long I was watching Robert saddle Dawn up. Wincanton is only a few miles from my parents' home, as well as being the nearest course to Robert's yard, so there was a large collection of Dorset friends and family there to watch. The ever-faithful Hils and Hugh had driven down from London, as had a friend of mine from Harvard, George Weston. Georgie and Richard Taylor and Michael Dangerfield were pleased that for once they had had a much shorter journey to the racecourse. Laurence and Barbara Tarlo were down in Dorset for the weekend, as were many of Robert's other owners, so there was no shortage of familiar faces in the crowd. It was great to see so many supporters, but at the same time I was very worried about making a fool of myself in front of everyone I had grown up with.

With ten minutes to go before our race, I waited just outside the men's changing-room trying to look and feel like a proper jockey. Yogi had drilled into me how well the professional jockeys rode and I was even more in awe of them all than usual. Several of the very top professionals were riding in our race, including the champion jockey Tony McCoy on the favourite James Pigg, and I was under no illusions about how talented they all were.

The Badger Beer Chase was one of the first decent handicaps of the season and there were a number of good fresh horses running. Carole's Crusader, ridden by Graham Bradley, had won two races already this season and looked like a promising graduate from novice company. In her last race she had beaten one of the other runners, the top weight Cherrynut. He was certainly no slouch. Also fancied was Baronet, a David Nicholson horse, who had been third in the Scottish National at the end of the previous season. In all there were nine runners and they were certainly the highest-quality group of horses I had ever raced against.

By the time Robert legged me up onto Dawn's back and Andy led us out of the course, I was so scared that I looked more like a petrified ghost than a jockey. I could see the Channel 4 cameras and I couldn't stop myself from wondering what on earth I was doing riding in such a high-profile race. As ever, Dawn took a ferocious hold going down to the start and at least I was able to focus on my familiar old fear of being run away with.

At the start, we circled for a few minutes and the professionals talked amongst themselves about who was going to make the running. I decided that rather than saying something stupid I would just keep quiet and listen. Brendan Powell saw me looking grim-faced and scared and smiled hello. He had schooled a couple of horses for Yogi while I was at Waterstock and he had admired Dawn then, so he took pity on me and he yelled out: 'Watch out everyone, there are two old grannies in this race – Dido and me.' It was the nicest way of saying to his fellow professionals: 'Beware, there's a lunatic about.' I was still smiling at Brendan's kindness when the starter dropped his flag and we were off.

I had never had to consciously start towards the back of the field before and I rather – no, seriously – mistimed it, leaving Dawn and me in last place rather than in the middle of the field. Tony McCoy set off at a fearsome speed on James Pigg and by the time we reached the second fence Dawn and I were several lengths behind the second-last horse and a good twenty lengths behind the leaders. Just as he had at home, Dawn didn't really attack his fences as much as I'd hoped and I wasn't confident enough to really drive him into them. After the first circuit we were well and truly at the back and Dawn just wasn't enjoying himself at all. Far from having trouble holding him, I couldn't get him to go fast enough. I think the reality was that both Dawn and I needed to feel the challenge of another horse beside to get into top gear. Tailed off at the back, Dawn was lazy and I wasn't brave enough. McCoy was still trail-blazing and we were almost a fence behind. Turning into the back straight the final time I jumped upsides Brendan, yelled hello and went past him. At least we weren't last any more. Down the hill towards the third last we caught Cherrynut and as we came into the finishing straight I realised how much running Dawn had to spare – he simply hadn't tried. A full fence ahead of us the race was really hotting up but Dawn and I were running in a race of our own. I was tempted to really push him over the last two fences to see how much ground we could make up but on second thoughts decided it would look even sillier to fall while riding a hard finish for sixth place. We crossed the line in seventh place with Dawn barely out of breath.

TOP: learning how to be an owner rather than a jockey (Les Hurley)
BOTTOM: Dawn fighting it out with Harwell Lad in the Betterware Cup at Ascot

Nervous but ready. Dawn and the two Andys before the start of the 1998 Cheltenham Gold Cup

Heart-stopping moments in the Gold Cup as Dawn leads throughout the first circuit *(top and above)*, but going into the last jump *(right)* Strong Promise has moved to the front (Anne Grossick)

Cool Dawn manages to find the extra stamina and speed needed to hold off Strong Promise and Doran's Pride to win the Cheltenham Gold Cup
(Anne Grossick)

Andrew soaks up the applause from the crowd *(left)* while Robert and I lead Dawn into the winners' enclosure (Anne Grossick); and *(below)* Andrew and Dawn look both exhausted and elated (Tom Lawrie)

The scoreboard shows the official result. Cool Dawn is the 1998 Cheltenham Gold Cup winner (Tom Lawrie)

Andy came rushing to meet us as we pulled up just beyond the stands and I don't think I had ever seen him look so glum. He took one look at Dawn and said: 'Hardly even tried, did he?' I think he meant me as well as Dawn. As ever when a race hadn't gone well, Robert and the fan club kept their mouths shut, but their faces told me all I needed to know. Dawn and I had failed our first big test – totally. John and I drove back to London in silence – there really wasn't anything either of us could say to make things seem better. What's more it was my birthday and I really was not in the mood for the celebrations back in London.

The only person who had a worse journey back to London was George Weston. He got lost along the narrow Dorset lanes around Wincanton and somehow managed to end up some fifty miles away in Bath before he realised he was heading west and not east. It was not a good introduction to the Cool Dawn fan club.

I knew things hadn't gone too well, but I wasn't really prepared for what happened next. At Wincanton after our race, Robert had said he wanted to run Dawn again as soon as possible and Dawn was entered in a race at Kempton in ten days' time. The day before declarations for Kempton Robert called. He had schooled Dawn himself that morning over fences at home and he really wasn't happy with the way Dawn was jumping. As at Wincanton, Dawn wasn't attacking his fences at all. 'Phew,' I thought, 'at least it's not just me.' But worse was to come. Robert didn't think I had the strength to sort him out and he wanted a professional to ride him to get him jumping properly. 'Then,' he said, 'of course you can have the ride back.' He also didn't want to run Dawn at Kempton because he wanted Andrew Thornton to ride him and Andrew was riding another Alner horse in the same race. Instead, Robert proposed that Andrew rode Dawn at Ascot on the following Saturday. 'Why don't you have a think about it,' he suggested, 'and give me a call back later today?'

I put down the phone not really knowing what to think. I'd

worked so hard trying to get good enough to keep the ride and suddenly it all looked in vain. I called Yogi to ask his advice and found him singing from the same hymn sheet as Robert. Yogi heartily approved of putting a professional on Dawn for one or two races to really get him going again. But he tried hard to reassure me that there was no reason why I couldn't go back to riding Dawn after that. He claimed that he had sorted out a number of event horses for amateur owners by riding them in one or two events and then returning them to their owner-riders much improved. It all sounded very logical, even if I didn't want to believe it was happening. Somehow this was very different from the Irish National. Then Robert had given me the option to ride, now he was not. Part of me was screaming that I owned the horse and paid all his fees, so why the hell shouldn't I ride him if I wanted? But another, more sensible, part of me found it hard not to accept Robert and Yogi's advice and risk ruining a brilliant horse. In the end, it went against the grain to ignore the advice of top class professionals like Robert and Yogi, so with a very heavy heart I called and told Robert to go ahead and book Andrew for Ascot.

One of the hardest things I had to do then was call the fan club and let them know the change of plan. It was like publicly admitting you had been fired by a company you owned! Everyone was very sympathetic but I got the distinct impression that my parents were quietly pleased that they would be able to enjoy a day's racing at Ascot without fearing for their daughter's life. On the other hand, Hils was worried that I would break her arm if I was anything like as bad as I'd been in Ireland and only promised to come if I didn't stand beside her during the race. They all agreed that they would be there to support me, even if the terrors of the day would be somewhat different from watching me ride. All in all, it was a day I was dreading.

One big difference between going racing as a jockey and as an owner hit me first thing in the morning. What does an owner wear to Ascot in November? I'd never really worried about what I wore, because once I had walked the course I changed into my racing kit. Ten years before I had been a spectator at Royal Ascot in June, but Ascot on a cold, damp and dark November Saturday was a rather different matter. After most of my suits had been discarded on the bed, I opted for grey trousers and a waist-coat with my long leather coat. I'm not sure I would have won the best-dressed award on Ladies' Day but the gatemen let me into the members' enclosure so it can't have been that bad. But it did feel very strange.

The fan club arrived in force, as promised. Hils and Hugh, Mum and Dad, John, and Georgie and her father were there as usual. A new addition to the group was Alex Thompson, Georgie's vicar's wife. She was a keen armchair follower of Cool Dawn and, although she would never admit to it, might even have won a penny or two on him as well. Everyone settled down for a lovely but pricey salmon and white wine lunch. It seemed strange to join the fan club in such a relaxed atmosphere, but for a moment being an owner didn't seem so bad after all.

It wasn't long before reality struck home. When Robert set off to put someone else's saddle on Dawn I realised quite how superfluous I was to the day's events. If I couldn't ride Dawn I would have been quite happy to be his stable lad for the day. But there were two problems with that. Firstly, it is not considered normal or, indeed, acceptable behaviour for owners of horses in valuable handicaps at Ascot to lead up and wash down their own horses. Secondly, and more importantly, I might have been fired, but Andy Miller had no intention of being. Andy rode Dawn at home when I wasn't there, and always accompanied him to the races. He had done a superb job at keeping Dawn calm and there was no way I dared take his place. Instead, my role was reduced to helping Robert saddle Dawn. I stood on one side of him, with Robert on the other side, as we strapped on Andrew's feather-light saddle. It wasn't much of a substitute for riding but at least I felt that I was a tiny part of the team.

Robert and I followed Dawn as Andy led him into the paddock and I started to eye up the opposition. There were only five runners in Dawn's race – the Gardner-Merchant Handicap Chase – which was run over the same three-mile course that Dawn and I had won over together two seasons before. The only difference was that that race was worth five thousand pounds and this one was worth a cool fifteen thousand pounds. The top weight was Coulton, a top-class horse probably at the tail end of his career. He was very high in the handicap and carried twelve stone. This put all the other horses out of the handicap with the minimum weight of ten stone. Dextra Dove was another Alner horse in the race, ridden by my friend from Wincanton, Brendan Powell. 'Dexie', as we all called him at home, had been a fabulous servant but was also reaching the end of his career. He was the only horse at longer odds than Dawn at 10–1. The favourite at 7–4 was Aardwolf, owned by Nigel Dempster (of the *Daily Mail*) and his wife. He had been a promising novice the previous season and was expected to make a successful transition to handicaps. The only other horse in the race was Glemot. I didn't spend much time trying to decide which horse was the most likely winner and, to be honest, all I cared about was that Dawn went well enough that I would be allowed the ride back next time. I certainly didn't think about him winning.

When Andrew came into the paddock and shook my hand it suddenly felt very formal and serious. Robert gave Andrew his instructions and kept to the story that he had told me: Andrew was to get Dawn attacking his fences and sort him out so that I could ride him next time. I grinned hopefully as Robert said that, but with hindsight I guess I have to ask myself how much he meant it.

As the horses left the paddock I started to feel a bit like I had in Ireland: scared. John was kind enough to let me borrow his binoculars as I had never bothered to buy any up until then because I was always riding. But, as the horses lined up at the starting line, I quickly discovered that my hands were shaking too much to be able to see much at all.

I had just got the binoculars to focus when the starter dropped his flag and they were off. Andrew kicked Dawn up into the lead as planned and really drove him into the first fence. He and Dawn landed in the lead and headed on down the hill with the other four runners strung out behind them. Dawn jumped the next few fences perfectly. I couldn't get over how quickly he and Andrew had clicked together. It certainly was a demonstration of quite how much better professional jockeys are than bumbling amateurs like me. At the open ditch in the back straight Aardwolf fell, leaving just three opponents for Dawn. By the time Dawn came past the stands with one more circuit to go, all three were still quite a way behind him and he seemed to have the race well under control. Andrew had him jumping so well that even my nerves were starting to calm a little.

They headed down the hill a second time and again Dawn jumped the downhill fences beautifully, bowling along still in front. Dextra Dove looked as if he was starting to lose interest and Coulton and Glemot still had a lot of ground to make up. Along the back straight I started to think they might win. The fan club did too and there were a few hesitant, 'Come on Cool's muttered into binoculars around me. As Dawn rounded the final bend, Glemot and Coulton came to challenge. All three horses jumped the second last in a line and the commentator clearly thought that the top weight, Coulton, was about to win. But Andrew crouched lower in the saddle and urged Dawn on, and within seconds Dawn was four lengths clear. As they accelerated into the last fence they looked to have the race won and we were all screaming on the top of our voices. At the last moment Andrew saw a long stride and urged Dawn to take off. Dawn disagreed, put in another stride and for a dreadful instant it looked as if they had both fallen. But Dawn had no intention of falling and somehow he and Andrew managed to haul themselves over the fence. They galloped away to pass the finishing-post some five lengths in the lead with Glemot second and a weakening Coulton third.

We couldn't believe it. They had won! I was so proud of my horse, it was incredible. I rushed over to Robert who was grinning at me and said happily: 'So, do I ride him next time?' I was expecting Robert to say yes immediately.

Robert just calmly looked up and said 'We'll have to see.'

I was absolutely elated that Dawn had won, but I suddenly realised that he had won too well. Apart from the last-fence blunder he had looked like a seriously good horse, in stark contrast to his performance with me. Robert was a professional trainer. It would be only human of him to want to have the best jockey on his horses and Andrew had just demonstrated the considerable difference in our respective abilities. I went to welcome in my Ascot winner with very mixed feelings indeed.

Andrew was grinning from ear to ear as he jumped down off Dawn. One of the first things he said to Robert and me was how sorry he was that he nearly mucked things up at the last. I think he was a little taken aback when I roared with laughter and said not to be sorry at all. I wouldn't have minded in the least if he had fallen off as then I would have had a cast-iron reason for demanding the ride back. Judging by the look on his face, that wasn't the response he had expected from an owner who had just won a valuable race!

When you win a race at Ascot, the racecourse give you a video of the race in a smart green case with 'Your Ascot Winner' embossed on the front. As soon as John and I got home I insisted that we watched the video so I could relive Dawn's victory. I was still feeling a little sore about not riding and I hoped that watching the race again would help me come to terms with how much better Andrew was as a jockey. Unfortunately, my mood was not improved one tiny bit by listening to the BBC commentary. Julian Wilson explained to the nation that I had given up the ride that day because I couldn't do the weight. I am only five foot two and if I couldn't ride at ten stone, I would look like a Teletubby. In fact my main problem is not weighing enough to be a good steeplechase jockey. Even on a horse set to carry ten stone I have to carry a stone and a half of lead in my saddle and lead weight is much more tiring for a horse than live, moving weight. When Yogi called that evening to congratulate us, I told him of this great insult and he only laughed and asked which I preferred: to be called too fat or simply too hopeless to keep the ride. I suppose he had a point.

The next week, negotiations began between Robert and me about who should ride Dawn in his next race. I was really torn in two. On the one hand, watching Dawn was just not as exhilarating as riding him myself. I had bought him to ride and although he could undoubtedly win a lot more money if professionally ridden, the money wasn't really the point. On the other hand, Robert felt Dawn could be a really first-class horse and I did not want to suppress a talented horse because of my own selfishness. If Dawn was good enough to make it to the top I didn't want to stand in his way. It was not easy to decide what to do.

In the end we hit upon what seemed like a sensible compromise. During the season Dawn would probably run in a couple of the top staying handicaps, but as there weren't very many of them he would also need to run in a couple of less-valuable races. I agreed to let Andrew ride him in all the big races on condition I could keep the ride for the smaller races. Robert and I set the ceiling at twenty-five-thousand pound races (above that Andrew rode, below I did) and we both started scouring the racing calendar for suitable races.

Robert found a fifteen-thousand-pound race in a fortnight's time and, for a moment things were looking good for me. Then I flicked through a couple more pages and found The Betterware Cup on 20 December. The Betterware was worth thirty-five thousand pounds so there was no escaping a difficult decision. Somehow, Robert had managed once again to persuade me not to ride. The Betterware was a really high-class handicap.The previous year's winner, Go Ballistic, had been fourth in the Cheltenham Gold Cup, so we would certainly get a better idea of how good Dawn really was. I consoled myself that if Dawn won, the owner's prize money was an awesome eighteen thousand pounds and if he didn't, then I would surely succeed in getting the ride back next time.

The fan club had been really rude about my old leather coat at Ascot, so the week before the Betterware I went to Harvey Nichols and spent some of Dawn's winnings on a ridiculously expensive cashmere coat. As a result I felt (and looked) a little bit more like an owner when I walked into the members' enclosure for our second visit to Ascot in a month.

I needed to look smart because Betterware Day is a very smart day's racing at Ascot. Held on the Saturday before Christmas, the Betterware is one of the biggest steeplechases that Ascot hosts and there was a large and extremely well-dressed crowd filling up the stands. It was hard to believe that Cool Dawn, my point-to-pointer, was running in such a prestigious race, and even harder to believe that other people thought he might win. He was ante-post favourite and even Chris McGrath in *The Times* tipped him to win.

The Cool Dawn fan club were doing their bit for Ascot's turnstiles and once again there was a large contingent to support us. New members of the supporters' club for the Betterware were Jono Holmes and Katherine Weston – George's wife. Together with Hils and Hugh, James, Laurence, George Weston, my parents and John, they all crammed into Ascot's seafood bar (a truly expensive way to get away from the bitter cold outside) and ensured that the caterers' takings for the day got off to a very good start.

Robert had several runners elsewhere that day, so Sally was in charge at Ascot. Dawn wasn't the only Alner horse in the Betterware – Harwell Lad and Rupert Nuttall were also running – so Sally and I had two horses to saddle before the race. We both get quite wound up with worry before a race and we obviously weren't a very good saddling team because as Harwell Lad was led round the paddock we suddenly realised that his number cloth was upside down. Sally and I had been in such a state that we hadn't noticed. In a panic we resaddled Harwell Lad in the paddock live on BBC. It did nothing for our nerves.

The whole fan club climbed up the stands to what was becoming our usual vantage point in the owners' and trainers' stand to watch the horses parade. I still could not really believe that Dawn was running in a premier race. There were only six runners but they were all high-class horses. Top weight was Unguided Missile, a horse trained by Gordon Richards. He had run in last year's Gold Cup and was rated only ten pounds lower in the handicap than the winner Mr Mulligan. Several years before Unguided Missile had beaten Dawn in one of his Irish point-to-points. Next in the weights came Go Ballistic – the previous year's Betterware winner. He had a lot more weight to carry than last year, but he was still a very serious contender. The next was Callisoe Bay. He had won his first two outings of the season and in his last had beaten Challenger du Luc, last season's Murphy's Chase winner and a favourite for the King George. He looked like he was a horse moving into the very highest echelons of steeplechasing. Then came Harwell Lad, Robert's Whitbread winner, who was owned by Dawn's old point-to-point trainer Harry Wellstead and ridden by Rupert Nuttall. He was on very long odds because of his highly unpredictable temperament, but there was no doubt that if he was so inclined he was a very good horse. Next came David Nicholson's Call It A Day. He had been a useful novice last season and David Nicholson wouldn't be running him in the Betterware if he didn't have a chance. And finally came Dawn. Bottom weight, but favourite. It didn't feel real.

My hands were shaking again as they lined up at the start,

but this time with a mixture of fear for Dawn and excitement; could he really beat such good horses – surely not?

The starter dropped the flag, Dawn and Andrew set off in the lead, as expected, with Harwell Lad second. The plan was for Dawn to stay on the outside of Junior to try and encourage him to race. All went to plan for the first circuit with Dawn and Junior sharing the lead both jumping effortlessly well. I was standing beside Harry Wellstead and it's very debatable which of us was more nervous as our two horses galloped past the stands for the first time side by side.

As they headed downhill away from the stands on the second circuit, Junior started to have second thoughts and for an instant looked like he was going to pull himself up. Somehow Rupert managed to coax him back into the race and, just as Junior was going forward again, Callisoe Bay made a disastrous mistake at the ditch and was out of the race. As Junior and Dawn accelerated round Swinley Bottom still neck and neck in the lead, Harry and I were speechless with excitement and worry. Over the next Junior went half a length clear of Dawn and they both drew well clear of Go Ballistic, Call It A Day and Unguided Missile. 'Looks like you've got us,' I said to Harry.

'It's not over yet,' came the tense reply, as they thundered into the next.

Over the last in the back straight Dawn drew level with Junior and then went a length ahead. None of the other horses was anywhere to be seen. Suddenly, Andrew was urging Dawn further and further ahead and Harry pointed out: 'Actually, it looks as if you're going to beat us.' Dawn jumped the second-last five lengths in front of Junior and came past the stands with nearly ten lengths in hand. We all held our breath as he and Andrew approached the last, they cleared it neatly and galloped past the finishing-post a clear winner. Rupert and Junior also took the last with ease and were a very creditable second. The rest of the field were nowhere to be seen. Harry and I hugged each other. It was a shame that one of our horses had to beat the other, but it was still an Alner one–two and between them they had decimated a high-class field.

I rushed down the steps of the stand with glee and ran out on to the course to greet Andrew and Dawn. It was an amazing victory; Dawn had beaten a field of top-class chasers and beaten them well. Andrew was over the moon, not least about clearing the last fence without a hitch. I led him and Dawn back into the winners' enclosure on cloud nine.

As Andrew went to weigh in, I was surrounded by a hoard of journalists. They all wanted to know how it felt to give up the ride and when I would be riding Dawn again. I can honestly say I didn't feel any resentment about not riding because it was so marvellous for Dawn to have won such a big race. I was so proud of him and in my heart of hearts I knew I would not have given him anything like the ride that Andrew had. I couldn't say I enjoyed watching him race as much as I did riding him, apart from anything else because watching was so much more stressful. I stuck firmly to my mantra that sooner or later Dawn would reach his level in the handicap and then I would be able to ride him in less valuable races.

After I had been presented with an extraordinarily large cup, I was invited to go up to Her Majesty's Representative's box for a drink. I asked if I could bring my family and friends and I don't think the Ascot officials realised what would happen when they said yes. The extended fan club numbered at least twenty and included all Harwell Lad's connections as well. We completely filled the box and downed all their champagne. We watched a replay of the race. Again the commentator, this time Richard Pitman, claimed the reason I wasn't riding was that I couldn't do the weight. The fan club booed him loudly. But the boos turned to cheers for both Alner horses as they pulled well clear of the rest. I think at this point the Ascot Officials might have begun to regret their invitation.

Next it was on to the stables to say well done to Dawn. It's quite a long trek from the course to the horseboxes. As Sally Alner and I fairly bounced down the hill towards the stables we started talking about Dawn's next race. Sally had been chatting to several of the jockeys when she had gone to collect the colours after the race and they had all been very impressed with Dawn's run. Graham Bradley had suggested that it might have been a Cheltenham Gold Cup-level performance and what's more Sally was taking his views seriously. I couldn't believe what I was hearing. Sally and Robert are always realistic about their horses, so for her to be talking seriously of the Gold Cup meant it must be a real possibility. For a split-second I thought that if Dawn was aimed for the Gold Cup I definitely wouldn't ride him next, but that irritation was quickly replaced with a sense of complete incredulity. My Cool Dawn might be capable of running in the Gold Cup. I fed Dawn his usual post-race Polos with a sense of sheer amazement. Sally couldn't really mean it, could she?

The next day, it wasn't just Sally who was talking about the Gold Cup. The papers were full of praise for Dawn's run and no one seemed to think it out of place to aim for Cheltenham. Incredible. There were several nice articles about my selflessness in giving up the ride which were nice to see. If I couldn't ride him at least the commentators seemed to understand how hard it was to stand back and watch.

One such article came from a very unexpected quarter and also helped to fill in a few gaps on the fan club's activities that day. Robin Oakley is a political correspondent for *The Times* but among other things also writes a racing column in *The Spectator* magazine. That week, his *Spectator* article was devoted primarily to Dawn and my dilemma over whether to ride him or not. He was very sympathetic, particularly about me being too short to make a good jockey. He was amused by the fan club teasing me by shouting: 'Stand up, Dido,' when I was clearly standing at my full height to receive the cup. He had also written of two men comparing the size of their mobile phones – in this case small is beautiful – something that they had apparently had a long conversation about instead of watching the next race. Pretending to be embarrassed, Hugh and Jono were delighted that their presence at Ascot had made the national press.

And so the Gold Cup dream started. At a time of year when small children go to bed imagining what Father Christmas might bring them, I was drifting off to sleep dreaming of what it might be like to have a runner in the Cheltenham Gold Cup.

Chapter Seven

The Build-up to the Gold Cup

To begin with, the Gold Cup was no more than a distant dream. Then, as Christmas came and went, I could see that Robert and Sally were taking it more and more seriously. Andrew broke off from a family Christmas in the north of England to fly down and ride See More Business, one of the Cheltenham favourites, in the King George on Boxing Day. Andrew's career took another major step forward with a tremendous victory live on national TV. He came back from that ride and told us that he would find it hard to split Dawn and See More Business in ability. Another signal that we weren't mad to be considering the Gold Cup.

Every morning in January, I sat on the train to Peterborough reading my copy of the *Racing Post* and watching out for comments about Dawn. On 13 January the *Racing Post* ran a feature previewing the two big championship races at Cheltenham: the Gold Cup and the Champion Hurdle. They reviewed each of the fancied horses and then made antepost tips. I scanned through the articles until I found the paragraph about Dawn. They were generally complimentary about him and not too rude about me, so I was reasonably satisfied until I turned over the page to read the summary. On the next page I saw a lovely picture of Dawn and Andrew jumping one of the downhill fences at Ascot and was absolutely astonished to see that Pricewise had tipped Dawn as the best ante-post bet for the Gold Cup. I was so excited I immediately whipped out my mobile phone to call Sally Alner, then my mother and then John. We weren't the only lunatics thinking of Dawn running at Cheltenham, some people seemed to think he might even win!

But there's a price to pay in all real-life fairytales; mine was to wave goodbye to the agreement that Robert and I had made about my retaining the ride in less valuable races. There was no question of my riding Dawn in his next race if the Gold Cup was seriously on the cards. Even if the race was worth less than twenty-five thousand pounds, Robert felt that it was far too important for Andrew to continue building a relationship with Dawn to have me stepping in for even one race. It was still only January and, increasingly, I felt I had nothing to lose. If Dawn and Andrew continued winning as they had, I stood a good chance of owning a Cheltenham Gold Cup runner, which was pretty awesome to begin with. There again, if Dawn didn't carry on improving, I was just a race or two away from getting the ride back permanently. Not a bad set of options whichever way you looked at it.

Robert and I again pored over the racing calendar and agreed a provisional plan. Ideally, Dawn would have two more races before Cheltenham, first at Ascot at the end of January and then in the Racing Post Chase at Kempton towards the end of February. On both occasions he needed to win, or come very close, to deserve his place in the Gold Cup line-up.

It wasn't long before we were all heading back to Ascot again. This time Dawn's race was on a Friday, in the strangely memorably named OK Soil Remediation Handicap Chase. The race was worth fifteen thousand pounds so, by our previous agreement, it should have been me riding. I managed to keep the thought of Cheltenham in my head every time I felt a pang of regret that it was Andrew's name on the racecard not mine.

The OK Soil was on a Friday, so, inevitably, it was a much smaller and more select group that gathered for smoked salmon and white wine in Ascot's now familiar seafood bar. Georgie and her father Michael had driven up from Dorset for the occasion, as had my parents. Hils and Hugh were there as ever, somehow they always managed to escape work for a day's racing, but everyone else claimed they had to work for a living and couldn't take Friday off.

The same seemed to be true for the whole Ascot crowd. The course was very empty and quiet compared to Betterware Day, and it was not helped by particularly dank and dull wintery weather. The going was described as sticky and dead and that rather summed up the atmosphere on the course.

Robert and I saddled up Dawn together in what was becoming a well-worn ritual and, as we followed Dawn and Andy Miller into the paddock, we started to consider the other runners. It was a very different race from the Betterware. Then Dawn had been bottom weight taking on some top horses. Today he was the top weight, every inch the Gold Cup contender out to stake his claim on the Blue Riband event of steeplechasing.

There were only three other runners, none of whom were being considered as serious contenders for the Gold Cup, and there was a lot of pressure on Dawn and Andrew to win, and win well. If they didn't our Cheltenham hopes would be pretty much ended for good. The other class horse was Go Ballistic. Dawn had beaten him easily in the Betterware but his connections claimed he hadn't been right then. This time he was carrying five pounds less than Dawn and had the added advantage of champion jockey Tony McCoy on his back. Next in the weights was Arfer Mole. He had won his last race at Kempton and Dawn had to give him nineteen pounds. The final runner was Orswell Lad who was ridden by a young Irish amateur called Robert Widger. Thanks to his handicap and his jockey's inexperience Orswell Lad would be carrying two and a half stone less than Dawn.

As Andrew and Dawn cantered down to post, for the third time in as many months the fan club climbed the steps into the owners' and trainers' stand and the race was on. I should have been getting used to using binoculars, yet somehow I still could not stop my hands from shaking. We seemed so close to the Gold Cup and yet it could all go up in smoke at any moment if Dawn didn't perform or he and Andrew came a cropper on any one of the numerous pitfalls of steeple-chasing.

From the start it was clear that Go Ballistic and Tony McCoy were not going to let Dawn and Andrew dictate things from the front. Down the hill towards the first fence McCoy drove Go Ballistic on until he was level with Dawn and continued to force the pace faster and faster. Dawn and Andrew would not yield and they jumped side by side for most of the first circuit with the other two runners trailing along some five lengths off the pace. They had covered the first mile and a half pretty quickly, but all four runners looked to be going well enough as they set off down the hill for the second circuit. From the stands everything seemed to be happening in slow motion. I had far too much time to think about what might go wrong. Had Dawn gone too fast for the first circuit? Could Go Ballistic keep this fast pace up?

Down the hill Andrew pushed Dawn on, but Tony McCoy and Go Ballistic showed no signs of giving in. Dawn had never been under this sort of pressure in a race before. Over the first fence in the back straight Go Ballistic looked to be getting a little tired, but he still had every chance as he and Dawn came side by side into the fourth last with Orswell Lad some six lengths behind and Arfer Mole already tailed off. Go Ballistic dropped his hind legs into the ditch, pecked on landing and McCoy went over his horse's head. They were out of the race. Dawn was some eight lengths clear with three fences to go and looked to have the race well and truly won. I started to relax until I remembered that Dawn and Andrew still had to jump three large Ascot fences.

Dawn had been going at a fearsome pace and as he rounded the final bend Orswell Lad, with two and a half stone less weight, looked to be getting closer and closer. I started to worry that we would get beaten, but I shouldn't have been so mistrusting. Andrew had just been giving Dawn a bit of a breather and although Orswell Lad tried to get on terms, Dawn was always going better and he crossed the line a clear winner by two lengths. We were safe and sound and surely Dawn had passed another test on his way to Cheltenham.

I rushed down to greet Andrew and Dawn and found both horse and rider breathing hard. Dawn had had a tough race and Andrew had had to ride him pretty hard to keep in front of Orswell Lad. Nevertheless, both trainer and jockey felt my horse had put up a pretty good performance, giving Orswell Lad so much weight on such dead ground. Andrew reckoned that he had heard Go Ballistic gurgle loudly going into the fence where he fell, a sure indication that the horse was starting to tire. He believed that had Go Ballistic not fallen, Dawn would definitely have beaten him. All this took us another step closer to Cheltenham, and yet another step further away from me riding Dawn in his next race. Robert wouldn't commit completely to Dawn running in the Gold Cup, but he would certainly be entered.

Once again we were all invited up into Her Majesty's Representative's Box for a drink after Dawn's win. On our third appearance we were greeted like long-lost friends by the Ascot officials and stewards. They were keen to find out if Dawn would be running at Cheltenham and were definitely on the fringes of becoming members of the Cool Dawn fan club themselves! I would like to think they were almost sad to see the fan club so depleted as it was on that Friday. I was certainly starting to feel at home as a winning owner at Ascot.

Cheltenham was now tantalisingly close to being a reality. Dawn would have just one more race and, provided that went well, the Gold Cup was on. But there was another unexpected problem on the horizon. A number of racing stables had been plagued all season with an equine flu that was proving very hard to eradicate. Soon after Dawn's last Ascot run, one of Robert's horses came back from the races with a very runny nose and it looked as if the stable had been infected with the bug. One by one the horses at Locketts were coming down with it. We couldn't afford Dawn to be out of action for several weeks when we were only six weeks or so away from Cheltenham, so he and Andy Miller went into isolation. One morning Sally told Andy to ride Dawn out of the main yard and not to come back, either of them, until the infection had cleared up. Dawn was to be stabled the other side of the farm as far away from the racehorses as possible. Andy exercised him on his own for over three weeks and neither horse nor rider were allowed to get anywhere near the other infected Alner horses. Every day we all worried that Dawn would have the dreaded bug, but after three weeks he still seemed in tremendously good health. It looked as if Sally had got him out of the main yard just in time.

Dawn needed just one more run before Cheltenham. Provided he ran well and the ground didn't get too heavy he would definitely run in the Gold Cup. Robert's original plan had been for that run to be in the Racing Post Chase at Kempton. John and I had carefully planned a holiday the week before so we could get some skiing in but still not miss Dawn's race. A few days before we were due to leave for our holiday, Robert called to suggest a change of plan. The Racing Post Chase was only twelve days before Cheltenham and he was worried that it wouldn't give Dawn enough time to fully recover. He had found a race at Sandown that suited Dawn in about a week's time, and wanted to know if I minded if Dawn ran there instead. I wouldn't have had any problems with the change of plan, but for the fact that the Sandown race was bang in the middle of our skiing holiday. I had learnt my lesson the previous year about putting my holiday plans ahead of Dawn's well-being so I gritted my teeth and agreed – on condition that Robert would give me a running commentary on his mobile phone so I could at least hear what was happening while I was far away in Canada.

John and I flew off to Canada while my parents and Hils and Hugh prepared to be the owner's representatives for the day at Sandown. John and I were staying in a chalet with six friends – including fan club members George and Katherine Weston. By the morning of the race everyone, including the chalet girl, had heard the hoof-by-hoof account of Dawn's racing career at least five times and we were all convinced that he would win. In fact, I think I had started to take winning for granted. I had even arranged with my mother that she should collect the cup when, or rather if, Dawn won.

The time difference between western Canada and the UK is eight hours. So, as Cool Dawn walked round the paddock at Sandown at three-thirty in the afternoon, John and I and the rest of our skiing party were munching our cornflakes and quietly recovering from the previous night's excesses at seven-thirty. As the horses went down to the start I rang Robert on his mobile for a stride-by-stride commentary of the race. It's not a cheap thing to do, calling a mobile phone for ten minutes from Canada, but – as ever – I needed to feel part of the scene, somehow. Even saddling Dawn up seemed a very integral part of the exercise in comparison to sitting in a kitchen talking to Robert on the phone over five thousand miles away.

Robert didn't tell me much about the other horses in the race – in fact I don't think I even knew at the time how many runners there were, he just focused on Dawn.

As the race started, Dawn and Andrew took up their usual place in the front and, according to Robert's commentary, they were jumping well and in the lead for the whole of the first circuit. I relayed the commentary to everyone else in the chalet kitchen and the tension started to rise. Several 'Come on, Cool Dawn's were muttered into binoculars in England and into cereal bowls in Canada. As Dawn powered down the hill away from the stands on the start of the second circuit he was still in the lead and everything seemed to be going to plan. 'Dawn's jumping the first fence in the back straight in the lead,' said Robert. Then the line went dead. In a complete panic I redialled his number and got a dead tone. I tried again and again but I couldn't get through at all. Everyone in the kitchen had stopped eating. Had Dawn won? We couldn't get hold of anyone at Sandown for ten minutes. In desperation I called Hugh's mobile instead and finally it rang. 'I'll put you through to Robert,' said Hugh instantly. What had happened? Had Dawn won? Robert came on the line. 'I'm afraid he didn't finish. He was overtaken at the railway fences and Andrew pulled him up and is cantering him back. I don't think he's lame but give me a call in ten minutes and I will know more.' I relayed the message to the rest of the kitchen with an ashen face. Suddenly the fairytale was over.

Ten minutes later, still shaking with fear and worry, I called Robert back. Dawn wasn't obviously lame or distressed. Andrew had reported that he hadn't been jumping with his usual verve. Dawn just hadn't seemed to be himself when he was overtaken in the back straight. Robert tried to reassure me that he would get to the bottom of what was wrong and not to worry. It was a bit late to suggest that. Our whole skiing party spent the rest of the day trying to distract me by making me ski down the most impossibly difficult slopes. If I wasn't careful both Dawn and I would be injured.

Back in England, the stewards ordered a routine dope test on Dawn because of his uncharacteristically bad run. Andy had to take him to the dope-testing box. As soon as Dawn relieved himself, the vets would take a sample of the urine and that should be that. Dawn didn't like this idea very much at all and, as a true-born stubborn scion of Over the River, steadfastly refused to do anything at all. Mum and Dad and Hils and Hugh likewise would not leave the racecourse until they had checked Dawn was all right and said goodbye. The four of them, plus

Robert, waited outside the 'dope box' as it started to get dark and Dawn still refused to pee. It was a full hour later, by which time it was very cold and dark outside, when the vet finally gave up waiting for Dawn and took a blood sample instead. All in all, I think it was a miserable day for every member of the fan club wherever we might have been.

John and I flew back from Canada a couple of days later and the first thing I did was to ring Robert for a detailed update. He was still not sure what had gone wrong. Dawn did not appear to be lame, seemed in good health and there were no signs of anything obviously wrong. Robert was waiting for the results of blood tests and two specialist horse physiotherapists were visiting that day. Hopefully he would know more in a day or so. The Cheltenham dream seemed to be fading away before our eyes.

Robert called me with slightly more reassuring news two days later. Both Sarah and Diana, the physios, thought that he had trapped a nerve in his shoulder. This would have made it hard for him to stretch out over his fences and to gallop at full speed. It looked as if, finally, we had an explanation. Dawn would start intensive physiotherapy immediately. It was still far from certain that he would make it to Cheltenham, but if Sarah and Diana worked miracles he might still stand a chance. We were back in business.

The countdown to Cheltenham started in earnest about ten days later when Dawn was given a clean bill of health. He would still have physio through the following few weeks before Cheltenham just in case, but he was able to go back into full work. Now all we had to worry about was the weather.

It had been raining hard over the previous week and the ground was starting to soften up. Dawn was definitely at his best on good and good to firm ground and really hated the mud. If it rained much more before Cheltenham the ground might well get too soft for him. Robert certainly didn't want to run him in the highest-class race of the year on very heavy ground. The fan club quickly developed a fascination with long-range weather forecasting.

With just three weeks to go before the Gold Cup, Sally also made a surprising request of me. She phoned up one Thursday evening and asked if I would mind taking Dawn hunting the following Saturday. She and Robert were obviously keen that Dawn was one hundred per cent ready for Cheltenham and they both felt that a day's hunting would do his mental health no end of good. It wasn't unusual for them to send a horse out hunting to sweeten him up before a big race, but I was very surprised that they wanted me to go with him. I was amazed that they considered me capable of keeping their precious Gold Cup runner under control out hunting. They obviously thought I had learnt something from Yogi. I wouldn't have missed the opportunity for the world and immediately said yes. I may have lost the ride on Dawn at the races, but at least I could still ride him in public out hunting.

The meet was on the top of Bulbarrow Hill at Delcombe Head, on the edge of the Dorset Downs just along the ridge from Robert and Sally's gallops. It was a lovely, sunny spring day and the green fields and hedges of the Blackmore Vale stretched out beneath us as we trotted up the hill to join the gathering field. Dawn loves hunting with a passion and both he and I were bursting with excitement as we arrived at the meet. He looked incredibly well, his coat gleaming with health and his muscles rippling with fitness. With his ears pricked and head held high, he looked every inch the equine superstar. The first person I saw was Patsy Harris, one of the Alners' neighbours and a first-rate horsewoman. At first she couldn't believe that I'd been allowed to take Dawn hunting either. When she got over the shock she was full of how exciting it was to have a Gold Cup horse out hunting with the Portman.

Within minutes everyone seemed to know who Dawn was, and one after another of the mounted followers came over to admire him. As I gulped down a glass of port, the foot followers also came to say hello to their local star horse. First someone came up and asked if they could pat him. Dawn loved the attention and arched his neck appreciatively as he was told: 'Now I've got 25–1 on you, so make sure you do your best.'

The next person told Dawn: 'Well, I've got 30–1.'

And so it went on. I was bursting with pride as we trotted off with the rest of the field to the first draw and Dawn's ego was being nicely massaged. I suspect this was just what Sally had been hoping for.

Dawn hadn't been hunting for a couple of years and age seemed to have made him a little more sensible. He was calm and well behaved for most of the day, though this might have been because the scent wasn't good and we didn't do much until late in the afternoon. Once the hounds did find though, Dawn was back to his old hunting self. The field was jumping a narrow post and rails with barbed wire underneath it and on either side. As soon as Dawn saw the horses jumping in front of him, he plunged forward, bucked and reared. Rather than fight him and try and avoid jumping the wire, I decided, perhaps a touch recklessly, that the safest thing to do was to let him jump the fence as quickly as possible. The atmosphere was electric as the entire field held their breath anticipating *their* Gold Cup horse being badly cut by the barbed wire. Dawn surged towards the fence and then leapt over it with complete confidence and apparent ease and the rest of the field were able to go back to concentrating on the chase. The spot is now known as the 'Cool Dawn rail' by everyone in the Portman Hunt.

As ever, jumping Dawn was exhilarating and, not to be deterred, we jumped the same fence a second time an hour later, this time going downhill at a fair speed. Dawn and I thought it was great fun, but Robert and Sally were less amused about our risk-taking when we got back. I have since had to promise never again to jump, go near or even look at barbed wire when riding Dawn out hunting. Despite their reservations about our bravery, Robert and Sally had to admit that the day's hunting had done him a lot of good. There was a real spring in his step when he went out on exercise the next day.

There was now less than two weeks to go before Cheltenham and there was very little I could do except worry. The main problem was still the weather. I used to lie in bed in the morning listening to the traffic going past our flat in central London, trying to work out if it had rained overnight and if there was water on the road. At work, I was splitting my time between Thomas Cook's retail base in Peterborough and the group's London headquarters. This actually meant that most of my time was spent travelling between the two places while making calls on my mobile phone. On several occasions I was talking to Mum, Georgie or Hils about the ground for Cheltenham while in the back of a taxi, only to find that the taxi-driver was a racing fan and wanted to know which horse I owned. I always insisted that they didn't waste any of their money on Cool Dawn because he wouldn't run if it rained, but I have often wondered since how many of them ignored my advice. All of them, however, were willing to add their views on the weather.

In addition to Dawn's new taxi-driving supporters, he also had a number of London Underground fans. Most mornings I set off for Peterborough via Covent Garden tube station. I always bought my *Racing Post* from Reg, the newspaper man who had his stand just outside the tube entrance. I had been doing this regularly for several years when a month or two before Cheltenham, Reg had asked me why I read the racing papers. It turned out that Reg and a number of the Covent Garden Tube Station crew were keen punters and from then on they became regular followers of Dawn. They too were watching the weather with a keen interest.

On the Friday before Cheltenham my owner's badges arrived. I was working from home that day so I was in the flat when the postman delivered them. When Dawn had run in the Foxhunters I had simply received four free tickets to the members' enclosure. This time, as he was running in the Gold Cup, as well as the four members' tickets, I had also been sent twelve passes that let friends and family into the owners' and trainers' bar, the paddock and, not that we would need it, the winners' enclosure. I knew to expect the extra badges but I wasn't prepared for what they would look like. They were circular beer mat-shaped cards with my racing colours and name printed on them, with 'Cool Dawn' and 'The Cheltenham Gold Cup' embossed around the edges. I sat there staring at them in amazement for ten minutes. This really was the top steeplechase in the world. I was desperate to share my excitement with one of the fan club. Hils works in Lincoln's Inn, only fifteen minutes' walk from our flat, so I called her and told her to drop everything and come and collect her ticket for Cheltenham. When she arrived we both just sat there and grinned like silly fools as it started to dawn on us that we really were going to the Gold Cup in a few days' time. It was the first time that I allowed myself to really believe that Dawn would run.

The next day, I was riding at the Seavington point-to-point in Dorset. The summer before I had bought a third share in a maiden point-to-pointer called Cardinal Gayle. The other two shares were owned by two keen members of the Cool Dawn fan club: Hugh and Alice. I rode Cardinal Gayle in his races, the two of them picked up any cups that we won, otherwise we split everything three ways. Cardinal Gayle, or Beamish, as we called him, was trained by Robert and Sally's daughter, Louise, who had just started a point-to-point yard of her own. He and I had had two runs before that Saturday, coming second on both occasions. For a couple of hours that day the Gold Cup was a very low priority in my life as I focused on race-riding once again, and everyone's hope that Beamish would break his duck.

The Littlewindsor course is everything that Cool Dawn would have hated. It typically has very boggy going in the early part of the season and has a number of sharp bends. Fortunately, Beamish loved these sorts of conditions and he had every chance in his division of the maiden race. It was all a very long way from racing at Cheltenham, but we felt very much at home. Hils's parents had come to watch, as had mine, and all the usual point-to-point crew were there including Michael Dangerfield, who was course inspector.

Beamish could not be more different from Cool Dawn if he tried. He is a small, compact horse who jumps sensibly rather than extravagantly. Unlike Dawn, he has always tried his best to follow every one of my instructions. This didn't stop me being nervous as we cantered down to the start, but I'm reliably informed that Beamish's approach to racing did a lot to calm the fan club's fears for my safety.

As is often the case in the West Country in March, there was an enormous field for the maiden and it seemed to take ages to check everyone's girths as we circled at the start. Cool Dawn even managed to intrude there when Tim Mitchell wished me luck. Of course, not for this race, but for Cheltenham instead. Tim was riding Fantus in the Foxhunters and hoped to win it for the second time in a row. I returned the good wishes and then we both started to focus on the important race in hand.

The starter moved up to his rostrum, dropped his flag and we were off. Beamish doesn't have a great turn of foot and I tried to get as good a start as possible. Inevitably, we were outpaced by a couple of speedier horses and lying sixth after the first fence. Beamish loved the going and jumped neatly and carefully as we came round past the crowd for the first time, though still in sixth place. Going out into the country, there was a long downhill stretch towards the start with no fences where we were able to make up some ground and by the time we had completed a full circuit we were nicely positioned lying third. Tim Mitchell had taken a crunching fall behind us at the open ditch first time. I could see him lying on the ground as we were rerouted around the side of the fence on our second circuit, but I was too focused on the race to think of the dangers. Beamish was still going well and we jumped up into the lead over the next fence as we came past the crowd. My plan was to start to stretch the field going downhill again and Beamish responded like the reliable, genuine horse he is, and we went down the hill as fast as we could. We were going so fast that Beamish was a bit too flat going into the next fence and he hit it hard in front. We lost a bit of momentum but were soon back into our stride. Our mistake had put Joe Tizzard and Smart Result back next to us. This was a well-fancied horse trained by Richard Barber and he looked to be going ominously well. I had the time between fences to think: 'Oh no – we're going to be second again.' We turned up the hill, bypassing the open ditch, and thank goodness this time Tim was standing up and looking in one piece after his fall. I didn't push Beamish up the hill towards the crowd, and all the time I expected Joe and Smart Result to come flashing past us. Into the final straight with only two fences to go and still we were in the lead. I urged Beamish on with all my strength, expecting to be overtaken at any moment but there was no sign of Joe. We jumped the last with three lengths in hand and crossed the line the clear winners. Beamish had finally broken his duck and we had won.

It might not have been a fancy Ascot hunter chase, but winning is winning, and absolutely nothing beats the feeling. Caroline Hinks and Louise led us back into the winners' enclosure, to find Beamish's co-owners Alice and Hugh grinning from ear to ear. It was the first winner I had ridden for two years and I was enormously pleased but I couldn't stop myself worrying that this might affect Dawn's chances. My first words to Caroline were: 'There goes my luck for the week. Dawn won't get to Cheltenham now!' I was convinced I had used up any luck I had that month with my thrilling ride on Beamish. Everyone was full of congratulations about our winning ride but the follow-up question was always the same: 'How's the other horse? Will he run on Thursday?'

Two days later, on Monday, I had another piece of tremendous good news. I was offered a very exciting new job. I had been approached by the Chairman of Thomas Cook's advertising agency to work with him. He was leaving his agency to become the European Managing Director of Manpower Inc. He wanted me to join him at Manpower as Managing Director of their UK operation. It was a tremendous opportunity and at that stage in my career it was well beyond my wildest expectations. I was completely overjoyed about it. My biggest concern was that this, together with my win on Saturday, surely used up all my luck and some. Something was bound to go wrong with Dawn before Thursday, but what?

On the Wednesday evening, the day before the big race, John and I were sitting watching the nine o'clock news when the phone rang. My first thought was that there must be something wrong with Dawn. But it wasn't that. It was my mother calling to tell us the good news that she *hadn't* won the midweek lottery! We weren't exactly expecting her to have won it and we didn't quite understand why she was so pleased that she hadn't. But she was convinced that good luck always comes in threes and what with Beamish's win and my new job she was very worried that our third piece of good luck would come before the Gold Cup. By now the whole fan club had reached a dangerous level of paranoia. Thank goodness there were only another eighteen hours to go before the off.

Chapter Eight

The Cheltenham Gold Cup

I didn't get much sleep the night before the Gold Cup and I woke up at about six in the morning terrified that overnight rain would have scuppered Dawn's chance of running. In fact, it looked like being an absolutely wonderful sunny day. Dawn was really going to run in the Cheltenham Gold Cup.

It now seemed very normal to be dressing for racing as an owner and I had no trouble deciding what to wear. My grey trousers and the long black coat I had bought with Dawn's winnings from his first win at Ascot were the obvious choice. As it was the Gold Cup, I thought I also ought to wear a hat. I thought about wearing my Cool Dawn baseball cap, but decided that it was a little too flippant. I did have a runner in the Gold Cup after all! Instead, out came the black felt hat I had bought to fend off the cold at Cheltenham two years earlier. We had had a great day then and maybe the hat would bring Dawn luck. I pinned on the special Gold Cup owner's badge and it all started to feel real – we were off to Cheltenham!

As I wasn't riding this time, John had persuaded me that it would be sensible to take the train down to Cheltenham so that I would be more relaxed (he hoped!). This would also prevent us from arriving at nine in the morning as we had for the Foxhunters. The plan was for John, Alice and me to take the racing special from Paddington that left London at around eleven o'clock and got to Cheltenham by one o'clock, in plenty of time for the first race at two. The rest of the fan club was driving to Cheltenham. Hils and Hugh had gone down the previous evening to stay with friends. Mum and Dad, Georgie, Richard and Michael Dangerfield drove up from Dorset. Alex Thompson had meant to come but her vicar husband had banned her because of a church lunch he was hosting, so Michael Dangerfield came on her ticket instead. Tom and Jill – my parents-in-law – drove down from Scotland the day before, while James Saunders had been propping up the bar at Cheltenham all week.

John had insisted on getting his hair cut that morning and as I was convinced he would miss the train, Alice and I set off by taxi to Paddington without him, having agreed that we would meet him at the station. Our journey got off to a bad start when our taxi was pulled over by a police motorbike for speeding coming off the A40. We had a good twenty minutes in hand before the train left but nerves were already well out of control and we were convinced that this hold-up would guarantee we missed the train. We obviously looked very distressed as the first thing the policeman did was try and calm us down and reassure us that we would be fine. 'Only if we get to Paddington in the next ten minutes,' was our response and before he booked the cabby the policeman kindly gave us directions to walk (or in our case run), to the station. We jogged nervously towards the station and predictably arrived with plenty of time to spare, to be followed a few minutes later by a freshly trimmed John, with that 'What were you worrying about time for?' look on his face.

The racing special from Paddington is a fantastic service. Great Western use all the old wood-panelled restaurant cars and the whole train is one very long restaurant car serving a cooked British Rail breakfast down to Cheltenham and a full three-course dinner coming back in the evening. The train gets in with plenty of time before the first race and leaves from

Evesham station an hour or so after the last race at the end of the day, to avoid the crowds at Cheltenham. It is a very civilised way of going racing and the train was crammed full of racing fanatics of all shapes and sizes.

As we got on the train I bumped into one of the waiters who normally worked on the London to Peterborough line. I often used to give him my *Racing Post* after I had read it and he greeted me with a grin and 'Will he win then?'. I still couldn't really believe that Dawn was going to run – winning hadn't even entered my head.

The train pulled out of Paddington and Alice, John and I settled down to read all the papers that we'd brought with us. As I read the previews of the race the butterflies really started to multiply. None of the papers seemed to think that Dawn had a chance. He was quoted at 25–1 by most of the bookies, but that didn't matter. I was still worrying about some last-minute hitch. I stared out of the window willing it not to rain, but the lush green countryside passed by without a cloud in the sky. It looked as if Dawn really might run. I could barely control my nerves. We ordered a big cooked breakfast and almost immediately I started to regret it. The three of us had one glass of champagne to toast the day but that was really more than my stomach could cope with. With each mouthful of breakfast I muttered 'I feel sick' to no one in particular. In the end John and Alice told me to shut up or stop eating. Everyone else around us was chatting loudly and preparing for a fun day at the races and they all must have wondered what on earth was wrong with me. The breakfast really was delicious and they naturally assumed that I must have been ill.

I think the stewards serving us were even more concerned when the table of four Irishmen behind us ordered their fourth bottle of champagne before twelve noon. I'm sure they were earmarked as the potential troublemakers for the journey home. Little did we all know what the journey home would be like!

The three of us arrived at the racecourse at one o'clock as planned and duly rendezvoused with the fan club and Robert. There was much excitement when everyone saw their special Gold Cup owners' badges – no one could believe it was all real. As before, our meeting point was outside Harriet Glen's jewellery stand. Harriet and her husband were both hard at work, but it was great to see familiar faces at the start of our nerve-racking day.

While the rest of the fan club went to get some lunch, Robert and I had to do a pre-race interview. There would be no walking the fearsome course for us today; instead we had to do our bit for the media. We fought our way through the seething crowds surrounding the weighing-room and found the Meridian TV crew. They wanted to interview both of us before the race about how we felt, but I think our grey, tense faces probably told the viewer more than our words ever could. We seemed to have come a very long way from our point-to-point roots and I think both Robert and I would have preferred to have been riding Dawn rather than watching him from the stands. Unfortunately, both of us had to grudgingly accept that Andrew would do a better job.

About half an hour before the Gold Cup was due to start Robert went to get Andrew's saddle. I left the fan club in the owners' and trainers' bar and went over to watch the Gold Cup horses, all seventeen of them, walk round the pre-parade ring. The pre-parade ring is a small oval path surrounded by railings around which the horses are led before being saddled up and taken into the paddock proper. It was a really lovely warm spring day and all the horses looked magnificently well with gleaming coats and bright eyes. Even at the pre-parade ring, there was quite a crowd eyeing up the runners in the country's top steeplechase of the year.

Many people outside racing think that the Grand National is the most prestigious steeplechase in the annual calendar, but for people inside the sport the Cheltenham Gold Cup is the race everyone wants to win. The Grand National is a handicap where horses carry more or less weight depending on their ability. It is a tremendously exciting and challenging race but it is not a test of which is *the* best horse over steeplechase fences, rather it is more a question of which horse gets the better of the handicapper on the day. The Cheltenham Gold Cup on the other hand is a level-weights race. All the horses carry the same weight, twelve stone, and the race is therefore a completely fair test of which horse is the best. The race is run over three miles and two furlongs, just like the Foxhunters we had competed in two years before, and only Europe's top steeplechasers enter the race. Trainers spend a lifetime trying to have a horse good enough to run in the Gold Cup, let alone win it.

As I stood watching the horses walk round in front of me, I could hardly believe that I was looking at such famous horses – let alone that one of them was my Cool Dawn. Doran's Pride, the favourite from Ireland, walked past me with two bodyguards either side of him – I had worried about a lot of things in the run-up to the race, but even I hadn't felt it necessary to employ bodyguards for Dawn. Richard Dunwoody was riding Doran's Pride, who had been third in the Gold Cup the year before in only his first season steeplechasing. The day before, the Irish had won the top hurdle race of the year, the Champion Hurdle, with Istabraq and they were hopeful that they would be taking both championships home with them for the first time in over forty years. Next came Barton Bank. Barton Bank had been second the previous year and I could remember watching him unseating Adrian McGuire at the last fence in the King George at Kempton live on television a few years before – surely my Dawn wasn't going to be running against such a famous horse? Then came the Hennessey winner Suny Bay, a big imposing grey horse who had been out of action since disappointing in this year's King George but, on his best form, was a marvellous horse. Following him was Strong Promise, an enormous black giant of a horse. Over two and a half miles Strong Promise was probably the best horse in the country. The papers didn't think he would stay three miles-plus but the horse was gleaming with good health and the firm ground would give him every chance of getting the trip. My eye then turned to See More Business. He was trained by Paul Nichols about two miles from my parents' house and was another West Country point-to-pointer, turned top-class chaser. See More Business had won the King George this year and was now second favourite for the Gold Cup after Doran's Pride – none of the pundits thought his West Country cousin Cool Dawn would beat him. The final horse that really caught my eye was Rough Quest. He had won the Grand National in 1996, as well as coming second in the Gold Cup that year, and was making a come-back after a leg injury. As the other ten runners walked on round the ring, I felt enormously honoured to be able to get so close to all these special horses. It was really hard to believe that Cool Dawn was amongst them. I must be dreaming.

Robert arrived with the saddle and the rest of the fan club and forced me to recognise that this was not a dream, it was really happening. Dawn was very quiet and calm as Robert and I saddled him up – was that a good or a bad sign? We were all too nervous to know the answer. Then it was time to follow my Gold Cup runner into the Cheltenham paddock.

For any normal race there is a small crowd of people inside the paddock consisting of an owner and trainer for each horse plus one or two friends. Then there is a slightly larger crowd outside the paddock leaning on the rails watching the horses. For the Gold Cup every horse had its maximum number of twelve human supporters in the paddock, plus various trainers, television crews, commentators and journalists. You could hardly move for people inside the railings, let alone outside them. From every vantage point around the paddock, people were craning their necks to get a sight of the Gold Cup runners. I guess that at least forty thousand eyes were trained on the horses as they walked round. The sun was baking down on us and it could easily have been July it was so warm – not quite the weather for a black cashmere coat and black felt hat. I was getting pretty hot underneath my owner's costume but I didn't dare take it off for fear of looking too scruffy. I think a number of the fan club were in the same position. We were all getting increasingly hot and bothered when John rightly pointed out that now Dawn was in the paddock and only minutes away from running it was time we started to enjoy the moment. We would probably never have another runner in the Gold Cup ever again and we should, he said, soak up the atmosphere. I looked around at the thousands of people and the course in the distance and tried to capture the scene in my head, so I would never forget it. None of us talked of the possibility of winning because we were all just coming to terms with actually being in the race at all. If Dawn came in the first six and therefore won a little bit of prize money we would be absolutely ecstatic.

Andrew came out of the weighing-room with the other jockeys and we had a quick chat about him and Dawn enjoying themselves. Within seconds he was on Dawn's back and Andy was leading them both out on to the track to parade with the other runners. The crowd was also piling away from the paddock and into the stands to get the best view they could. We had to decide where we were going to watch the race. Robert's first plan was not to watch the race from the stands at all because of the enormous crowds but instead to stay where we were in the paddock and watch the race on the big screen behind the stands. But the sun was too bright and it was impossible to see anything on the screen at all. By the time Robert and I had worked that out, the rest of the fan club had dispersed into the stands. Hils, Hugh, Alice and the three Dangerfields fought their way up to the top of the owners' and trainers' stand. James watched the race with some friends of his near the rails and Mum, Dad, Tom and Jill couldn't find the rest of us at all so watched the race in the Lawn Bar. Robert, John and I couldn't see any of them anywhere, so we forced our way up through the sea of people in the owners' and trainers' stand and found a tiny bit of space about halfway between the ground and Hils and Hugh.

Just as I was trying to focus my binoculars with shaking hands, I heard someone shouting my name. About twenty steps below us was Becks, one of our skiing party from Canada, jumping up and down like a pogo stick, yelling: 'Good luck – my money's on him.' I just had time to yell back hello when the commentator announced that they were off in the 1998 Cheltenham Gold Cup. The horses set off at a gallop and the crowd let loose the thundering Cheltenham roar.

My hands were shaking so much with excitement that I had no hope of seeing anything with my binoculars at all. Neither Robert on my right nor John on my left seemed to be having the same problem so while they trained their binoculars on the runners approaching the first fence, I alternated between watching the big screen on the other side of the racecourse and my feet. My feet seemed much the least stressful choice.

I heard rather than saw that Dawn had jumped the first fence in the lead. Barton Bank was just behind him, then came Senor El Bettruti and Suny Bay with the rest of the seventeen runners trailing out behind him. I looked up and saw Dawn jump the next fence in front of the stands with ease and set off downhill towards the third. He was still in front. He jumped the third fence perfectly and seemed to be running well within himself. There were no fallers yet and most of the other horses seemed to be going well too. There was still a long way to go. Neither Robert, John nor I said a word and I think the rest of the fan club was equally silent with worry in their respective vantage points as Dawn approached the first ditch. My old fears of Dawn hurting himself reappeared – please don't break a leg – I prayed as he took off. But I needn't have worried. Dawn and Andrew jumped the fence perfectly and headed on to the next still in the lead. They were leading the field a merry dance as they climbed up the hill towards the seventh fence. Dawn jumped it well and went another length in front and suddenly there was a commotion at the back of the field.

The commentator announced that See More Business had been carried out along with Cyborgo and Indian Tracker. In fact, Cyborgo had hurt himself and in a desperate attempt to avoid jumping the next fence his jockey Tony McCoy had pulled him sharply to the right and across the path of Indian Tracker and See More Business. Both horses had missed the fence and were out of the race. Robert and I looked at each other, both of us thinking that Dawn stood a better chance of a place without See More Business in the race, but neither of us wanting to be so uncharitable as to say it. That sort of bad luck could so easily have happened to us.

We didn't have much time to dwell on See More Business's fate and it was back to the race. Dawn and Andrew were jumping boldly over the two downhill fences, still looking to have everything under control. As they came past the stands for the second time all I could think of was that at least Dawn was in the lead for part of the race so that we would see him on the television highlights in the evening. Dawn led the field away from the stands downhill towards the next fence still with Barton Bank second and a tiny part of me started to think that he might have a chance of a place. Everyone in the stand was silent but you could tell they were all rooting for their horse. Dawn met the water jump wrongly but didn't lose momentum and he and Andrew were once again approaching the open ditch in the lead. Dawn measured it incorrectly and almost landed in the middle of it. I swore violently and couldn't watch. But Andrew was still driving Dawn on in the lead and they hadn't lost any momentum. Behind them, the other horses were starting to build up ready to make their challenge and people in the crowd were beginning to call quietly for their horses. Barton Bank was starting to fade but Doran's Pride looked to be going very well a few lengths behind Dawn. Beside him was Suny Bay and Strong Promise was looming up just behind them. As the horses climbed the hill at the top of the course, I was watching the big screen as it switched to show an aerial shot – Dawn was still three lengths in the lead. Surely he couldn't keep the lead for much longer. He and Andrew thundered down towards the third last still in the lead but with Doran's Pride and Strong Promise both getting closer and looking to be going dangerously well. If we're lucky he'll be third I thought, but surely that was too much to hope for. At the third last the commentator also thought Dawn wouldn't win and yelled: 'And here comes Doran's Pride,' but the favourite hit the top of the fence and sprawled on landing. The Irish in the crowd groaned when it looked as if their horse has missed his chance. Just as they said farewell to their money, the Cool Dawn fan club started to think we might just have a tiny chance of winning.

Into the finishing straight with only two fences to go, Dawn was still in the lead. My brain was saying, 'He can't win,' while my heart was screaming 'Go on, Dawn – you can do it.' Over the second last and Strong Promise still looked to be going incredibly well only half a length behind Dawn. Doran's Pride was fading, two lengths away, and the rest were nowhere. We could definitely get second and second in the Gold Cup would be absolutely incredible. I couldn't believe what I was seeing.

Over the last, Dawn and Strong Promise were neck and neck; perhaps Strong Promise was in the lead, I wasn't sure, because I was looking at my feet again. Andrew hit Dawn twice with his stick – the first time Dawn had ever been hit – and it was as if the horse understood what the Gold Cup meant. He instantly changed up another gear and started to accelerate once more. Strong Promise suddenly wasn't looking so comfortable beside Dawn. We all suddenly realised that Dawn might win, that he was going to win. Robert, John and I screamed on the tops of our voices:

'COME ON, DAWNNNNNN!' Across the course all the Cool Dawn fan club were yelling as loud as they possible could: 'GOOO OOOONNNNNN, DAWWWWNNNNN.' Dawn and Andrew gritted their teeth and went one, then two, lengths clear of Strong Promise. There was no doubt we were going to win. Dawn and Andrew flashed past the winning-post clearly in the lead with Strong Promise just holding on to second from Doran's Pride finishing with a late flourish.

I couldn't speak for all the emotion that was running through me. Robert hugged me and together we both burst into tears. 'Hey! That's my wife you're holding,' said John who was also beaming from ear to ear with a few tears in his eyes and all three of us hugged each other. There were similar scenes wherever the Cool Dawn fan club was gathered. The losing connections in the stands patted us all on the back as we climbed down through the sea of people. At the bottom I found Becks pogo-sticking up and down as if her life depended on it. She had won over one thousand pounds on Dawn. That was the first time it occurred to me what my prize money was. Oh my God – I had just won one hundred and ten thousand pounds.

My next thought was that I simply had to get down to the course to lead in Andrew and Dawn. Robert had the same idea but we were surrounded by a seething mass of people making their way to the bars, the bookies and the paddock. Robert led the way and we rugby tackled our way through the crowd, ducking and diving until we had fought our way to the walkway that leads out on to the course. Dawn, Andrew and Andy Miller were nowhere to be seen because the organisers always make the Gold Cup winner wait to be led in last to give the connections time to get back to the paddock – we needn't have rushed at all. But how were we to know?

Andy had run on ahead to collect Dawn and Andrew as they walked past the stands. I think the crowd was a bit stunned at a 25–1 winner but Andrew stood up in the saddle and encouraged them to cheer the 1998 Cheltenham Gold Cup winner. Dawn heard the crowd start to cheer and despite being exhausted from running the race of his life, he pricked up his ears, raised his head and tail and took the applause he somehow knew he deserved.

Finally, Andy, Andrew and Dawn appeared at the end of the walkway and Robert and I took either side of Dawn's reins and led him into the winners' enclosure. We were surrounded by thousands of people, with television cameras broadcasting live about four feet in front of us, but all I saw was my amazing horse.

We walked into the winners' enclosure to find the entire fan club virtually speechless for the first time in their lives. Robert gave Hils Dawn's sweat rug – he wouldn't need it now as he would be wearing the winner's rug – and Hils hugged it as though her life depended on it. My secretary from Thomas Cook, Fee, had somehow managed to squeeze her way to the rails of the winners' enclosure and was screaming: 'Well done, Cool,' at the top of her voice. We all hugged each other, grinned like fools and fought back the tears.

Within seconds of arriving in the enclosure, Robert, Andrew and I were surrounded by a crowd of journalists ten deep with microphones, television cameras and tape recorders. 'What was it like to remove the owner from her own horse?' 'When did you know how good he was?' 'Do you regret not riding him?' 'What does it feel like to win the top steeplechase in the world?' 'Will you ride him again?' In other circumstances it would have been terrifying to have one microphone after another thrust at you, but we had just won the Cheltenham Gold Cup and didn't care who wanted to talk to us about it!

I was just surfacing from the last of the interviews when Mum yelled out: 'Smarten up, Dido, the Queen Mum's coming to present the Cup.' I hadn't realised that the Queen

Mother was even at Cheltenham that day, let alone that she would be presenting me with the Gold Cup. But she had more important things to do first. She wanted to see the Gold Cup winner close up for herself. Andy had the five most terrifying minutes of his life as he held on to Dawn while the Queen Mother stood as close to him as she could. Dawn was restless and a little nervous of all the crowds and could very easily have knocked her over.

Then it was time for the presentation. I went up first and did my best impression of a curtsy, followed by Robert and finally Andrew. Andrew took the Gold Cup itself and held it up for the crowd to see. They gave him an enormous cheer. He had given Dawn the most brilliant ride and, much as I would have loved to have been in the saddle myself, I couldn't have asked for a better jockey.

I was just starting to look around and soak up the atmosphere when Peter Jones, who is the Chairman of the Tote, asked if I would like to join him for a drink in the Royal Box. As I had at Ascot, I explained about the fan club and he reassured me that everyone would be welcome. I guess he hadn't heard of our antics at Ascot. It took quite a time to fight our way through the crowds and up to the Royal Box and all the time I just couldn't get to grips with what had happened. Part of me just wanted to find a small corner to sit down and cry. I couldn't cope with all this emotion. Before I knew it, I was coming out of the lift into the Royal Box and giving my second curtsy of the day to the Queen Mother. With the fan club and the royal party there wasn't much room in the box. It was so cramped that Hils actually managed to stand on Princess Anne's toe as she jumped up and down cheering in the winner of the next race! We watched the Foxhunters from the balcony of the box and cheered for all we were worth when another Dorset horse, Earthmover, ridden by Joe Tizzard, came home the easy winner. At this point the powers that be decided that the Cool Dawn fan club had been in the box quite long enough!

The Cheltenham officials were incredibly helpful and they decided that we were clearly too delirious to be left on our own. Rather than leave us to find our way to the owners' and trainers' bar they took us to a room in the weighing area to watch the video and drink champagne. We filled the Gold Cup with fizz and passed it round with stupid grins on our faces. There, we were joined by Andrew and his girlfriend Gill. Andrew was proudly sporting Hugh's Cool Dawn baseball cap and was now a fully paid up member of the fan club. He and I watched the video, talking the race through stride by stride, and I couldn't get over the fact that although he had only ridden Dawn five times he definitely knew Dawn as well as, if not better, than I did. Next, Richard Pitman, the television commentator, came to apologise for claiming that I weighed more than ten stone. A very clever time to apologise, as I was so high on the emotion of the day that there and then I didn't mind what he had said about me. Next through the door was Yogi, grinning for all he was worth. Cool Dawn must be the only horse Yogi has helped get to the top by removing his jockey – quite an achievement really. The Cool Dawn fan club was growing with every passing second and consuming more and more champagne.

An hour or so after our victory the booze was starting to run out and I thought it was time I went to visit the star of the day. Andrew, Gill, Yogi and Richard Pitman went to rejoin their parties and the rest of us followed the hoofprints back to the racing stables.

In theory, members of the public are not allowed into the stables during racing but no one was going to stop the jubilant Cool Dawn fan club brandishing the Gold Cup in front of us. We found Dawn and Andy both quietly recovering from the stresses and strains of the day. Dawn was under no illusions about how special he was – and Andy certainly didn't disagree with him. Andy was proudly sporting a Cool Dawn cap – one which had started the day on Hils's head. Dawn could definitely sense the joy and elation in the atmosphere and was on top form. He munched through several packets of polos – including one fed to him in the Gold Cup itself.

In all the excitement we had lost Robert. All of a sudden we heard his name being given out on the tannoy by the racecourse commentator together with Princess Anne's. Robert had won the Guinness 'Pure Genius' Training Award for his outstanding performance in training Dawn. He was given an absolutely beautiful cut-glass vase that was richly deserved. Another large pot would be finding its way to Dorset that evening!

By then it was almost five o'clock and it wouldn't be long before our train would be due to leave. We fleetingly thought about hiring a helicopter to take us back to London, but not one of the fan club had the faintest idea how to go about it. Someone else suggested staying in Cheltenham and all going out to dinner but the racecourse officials advised against it on the grounds that we might have just won the Gold Cup but several thousand people had made dinner reservations several weeks before us. So we decided to make our way back to London and meet for a late dinner there.

The special racing service was heading back to London after the three days of the festival. So John, Alice and I bade farewell to the rest of the fan club and to Dawn, Andy and Robert and boarded the courtesy bus that would transfer us to Evesham Station. I was carrying a large hatbox, inside which was the Cheltenham Gold Cup. I was completely elated and longed to yell out to everyone else on the bus: 'Do you know what I've got in here?' It didn't seem a very sensible or a very practical thing to do, however. Instead, I sat on the bus, listening to everyone around me discussing how good or bad their respective days had been, all the time grinning to myself knowing that no one's day could have been better than mine.

The bus arrived at Evesham about half an hour before our train was due to depart for London and the bus driver suggested that everyone went to the pub at the end of the road to wait. John, Alice and I were starting to feel the stresses of the day. We were incredibly hungry and dehydrated from all the champagne. We pushed and shoved our way through the pub, which was heaving with drunken punters, and quietly ordered three Cokes and two packets of salt and vinegar crisps – not so much a celebratory drink as a restorative one. We put the hatbox with the Gold Cup inside it on top of a barstool and stood in a circle around it, protecting it from marauding drinkers. Not that anyone in the pub would ever in their wildest dreams have imagined what was inside our precious box. We didn't talk very much – the pub was getting pretty rowdy and it didn't seem too sensible to announce that we had the Cheltenham Gold Cup in a hatbox beside the bar. We would probably never have seen it again. Instead all three of us stood quietly nursing our Cokes and reviewed the race over and over again in our heads. Could it really have happened to us?

Before long it was time to catch the train. Hugh called on his mobile to tell us that he had booked a table for dinner at Langan's in Central London for ten o'clock. It was only six o'clock and I was already exhausted but I agreed we would see him there. We could always sleep on the train. In the meantime, Hugh and Hils drove back to town calculating just how much of their kitchen Mr William Hill would now be paying for. Certainly Hils could hardly carry the huge bundle of notes that they took from the on course bookies!

The train chugged in, and leaning out of the first window was my friend the waiter from my regular Peterborough train. He was grinning almost as much as I had been earlier and yelling: 'Well done – I knew he'd do it – we all had money on him!' It was pretty obvious I wasn't going to get much sleep on the train. We got into our carriage and our waiter greeted us with a bottle of champagne on the house and then picked me up and hugged me for good measure. There was no way we'd keep the Gold Cup secret here.

Somehow this was just the tonic I needed. All of a sudden I wasn't feeling so tired any more – there's no doubt that champagne is a much better pick-me-up than diet Coke. The three of us sat down at our table and with great ceremony opened the hatbox and got the Gold Cup out. Not all the carriages fitted on to Evesham station and so lots of passengers had to walk through our carriage to get down to their own. As each person walked past our table they couldn't miss the glittering gold cup sitting in front of us. Some people just grinned at us, but several said: 'Had a good day? What's that?' Safe in our carriage we didn't hesitate and shouted out triumphantly: 'It's the Cheltenham Gold Cup.' At first, our fellow passengers didn't believe us but the waiters soon set them straight. We were all going to have one hell of a party getting back to London.

Once the train was on its way and everyone had been served with a drink, the procession of visitors started. One guy from the table two ahead of us came over to see if it was true that we had really won the Cheltenham Gold Cup. 'Sure we have,' we grinned, 'why don't you have a drink out of it, if you don't believe us!' So, he duly drank champagne from the Gold Cup, grinned to himself and went back to tell his friends. Two minutes later all his friends were back at our table. 'Our mate tells us that you won the Gold Cup, so we wanted to see if he's drunk and hallucinating.' They each had a sip of champagne out of the cup themselves and went back to spread the word. From Evesham to London the Cheltenham Gold Cup acted as a veritable communion cup for the racing fanatics on the train (including most of the editorial staff of the *Racing Post*). We had a never-ending queue of passengers at our table each wanting to touch it, drink from it and hear the tale of Cool Dawn.

The table of Irishmen behind us who had had four bottles of champagne before noon were as drunk as you might have expected by eight in the evening. They were particularly cross with me for not giving them a tip on the way down but once they had had their chance to drink out of the cup they soon calmed down. One of them even asked me to say hello to his father who was on his mobile phone in Dublin! It was incredible how pleased everyone on the train seemed to be. I don't think anybody could believe that the cup was going back to London on the train rather than in a helicopter or a Securicor van. Even the train manager himself got into the act and had a photo of himself and me standing either side of the cup. You've heard of the people's princess, well this was very definitely the people's Gold Cup!

When the train finally drew into Paddington, the train staff were a bit worried about press being there to meet us and insisted that we wait to be escorted off the train by the police. In fact, there was nobody from the press there to greet us but nevertheless I carried the Gold Cup in front of me as I got off the train with two bemused policemen either side of me and got a rousing cheer from all my fellow passengers. The day was becoming more and more like a Hollywood fantasy.

Hugh and Hils had got back to London ahead of us and Hugh had thoughtfully come in a taxi to meet us at Paddington and take us to Langan's where the celebrating continued. We were joined by Jono Holmes and his wife Suzi, neither of whom had been racing and they were probably the only sober members of our party. We were tossing the Gold Cup round the table in a rather cavalier way when Jono asked what it was made of. 'Well, it can't be gold,' I said 'because I get to keep it. It must be plate at the very most.'

Suzi, who knows a bit about precious metals and was sober enough to find and read the hallmark had a look and calmly replied: 'No, it looks as if it's solid gold to me.'

'But we fed Dawn polos out of it earlier today,' came the drunken chorus from the rest of the table. We were all far too inebriated to remember whether we had even bothered to wash it out!

By eleven thirty we had all had more than enough food and champagne and the Channel 4 highlights were due to start on television. Langan's isn't far from Covent Garden and it seemed sensible to walk to our flat rather than wait for a taxi. Sensible, that is, if you have been drinking champagne since four in the afternoon. We all happily walked through some of the dodgier areas of Soho with Jono dangling the Cheltenham Gold Cup from his hand. But we were quite safe – who on earth would have believed what had happened to us that day, we certainly didn't.

The last of the fan club went home at one o'clock and John and I flopped drunkenly into bed. It had been the most incredible day but somehow I managed to look John straight in the eye, or at least as straight as you can after that much champagne, and say: 'This has been the most amazing day, but not quite as special as our wedding day.' It's a good line – but did I believe it . . .

I didn't get much sleep the night after the Gold Cup partly because of the alcohol working its way through my system and partly because my brain simply had not caught up with what had happened. I woke up at six in the morning and lay in bed wondering if it had all been a dream. Surely Dawn could not have won? I crept out of bed and went to check if the Gold Cup really was in our sitting-room. And there it was. I sat on the floor, holding the Gold Cup and cried my eyes out.

Chapter Nine

What Next?

S o what do you do with the rest of your life after you have won the Cheltenham Gold Cup? The answer is – try and win another race. Dawn might have won the biggest race of the season but before we thought about the rest of our lives there was still the rest of the season to complete.

Several weeks before Cheltenham, Dawn had been entered for the Whitbread Gold Cup, the same race that Harwell Lad and Rupert Nuttall had won the year before. The Whitbread is a handicap and the weights are set soon after entries are made in February and long before the result of the Cheltenham Gold Cup is known. As a result Dawn was set to run off a handicap twenty-two pounds lower than his post-Cheltenham mark. He would never again carry such a reasonable weight in a handicap. The last horse to win the Cheltenham and Whitbread Gold Cups in the same season was Arkle, a true racing legend. Could Cool Dawn win his place in racing history too? It was tremendously tempting to run him.

Dawn had had a hard race at Cheltenham, but he seemed to have recovered and was working extremely well at home. He was certainly aware that he had done something special and was brimming with self-confidence. It seemed crazy to keep him at home in his stable when he stood such a good chance in the Whitbread. Robert, Andrew and I were all keen to run him.

The Whitbread is at the end of April, a full month after Cheltenham, and you would have thought that the weather would be better than in March. But 1998 was a very strange year in more ways than one. While mid-March had been warm and summery with good or even firm racing ground, April brought torrential rain, grey days and increasingly soft ground. The Whitbread Gold Cup is run over three miles and five and a half furlongs – some three furlongs further than the Gold Cup – and with soft ground as well, Robert was worried that Dawn would not stay the trip. It looked as if Dawn might be prevented from running by the rain. Robert reconfirmed Dawn's entry the day before with a clear warning to the press that he would not run if it rained again over night. We had all thought that the weather might prevent Dawn from running at Cheltenham. We had managed to escape it then, but it looked as if the weather was catching up with us. I went to bed that night straining my ears for sounds of raindrops.

When I woke the next morning there was no doubt that it had been raining in central London. I could hear the water sloshing around on the road as the cars raced past our window. Sandown Park is in south-west London some five miles from our flat, so I was fairly certain that it must have rained there too. I rang Robert at seven o'clock, expecting him to say that Dawn wouldn't run but found him surprisingly upbeat. He had just spoken to the Clerk of the Course at Sandown who said that they had had no overnight rain at all. The rain must have been very localised indeed. Robert wanted to bring Dawn up to Sandown and walk the course himself before he made a decision. We were definitely going racing but it was far from certain that Dawn would run. It's what you call real-time decision making.

The fan club found this last-minute decision making hard to cope with and consequently many of them decided that they would watch the race on television instead. When John and I arrived we were met by my parents and my mother's half-sister, Lindy. The Cool Dawn fan club numbered only five – the lowest turnout ever. But there was another reason for the poor turnout. Beamish, the point-to-pointer Hugh, Alice and I owned together, was due to run in a point-to-point that afternoon. He had been bought so that I could ride him, but it was approaching the end of the point-to-point season and we were all keen for Beamish to have as many runs as possible. As Robert and I had been unable to decide whether Dawn would run, Alice, Hugh and I had agreed that Beamish would go to Larkhill whatever happened – and I would have to choose betwen riding and watching.

At the beginning of the 1997–98 season I would never have imagined that I would give up the chance to ride in a race in order to put on my smart clothes and go and watch a race from the stands. I did seriously consider hiring a helicopter, but Beamish and Dawn's races were only half an hour apart and there was no way I could be in both places in time. I had to choose between them. Much as I wanted to ride Beamish, I knew that there would be other races for him but that in all probability I would never again own a horse that stood a chance of winning the Cheltenham and Whit-bread Gold Cups in the same season. I suppose I had finally completed the transition from rider to owner – there was no doubt in my mind I had to be with Dawn. Beamish would run without me with ex-champion lady rider Alison Dare in the saddle and Hils, Hugh and Alice had gone to Larkhill to support him.

While the depleted fan club enjoyed Whitbread's hos-pitality and consumed a first-rate lunch, Robert and I set off to walk the course. Robert carried a large umbrella which he jammed into the ground every few feet to test how soft it was. We set off down the hill away from the stands and almost immediately we could hear the tell-tale squidging sound of wet ground as our feet sank into the mud. Approaching the downhill fence the spike of Robert's umbrella completely disappeared and we had to admit that just there the ground was definitely very soft. But we were both keen to run and we tried hard to persuade ourselves that such a small soft patch wouldn't bother Dawn. Next, we walked along the long back straight towards the railway fences. It felt very strange to walk the course with Robert and not discuss my riding instructions – maybe I hadn't completely forgotten what it was like to be an owner–rider. The ground along the back straight was better and although Robert's umbrella still went in a few inches, we both knew that we could convince ourselves it was okay. We climbed the steep hill towards the finish rehearsing our arguments for running Dawn. Channel 4 were keen to interview us on the course and we could see them waiting by the last fence. We had to make up our minds. It seemed very cowardly to withdraw when we were so close. Dawn had so much weight in hand we surely had to give him a chance. Even though the ground was against us, we would run.

I helped Robert saddle up Dawn as usual, but unlike Cheltenham I didn't feel in awe of the other horses. There was a large field – some twenty runners – but only two of them, Go Ballistic and Yorkshire Gale had raced against us in the Gold Cup. Dawn was now the highest-rated staying chaser in the country and good though the rest of the horses were, we knew we deserved our place in the line-up. Despite the ground Dawn was still a short-priced favourite at 5–1 and he looked absolutely superb. His summer coat had come through and shone like a mahogany table. He certainly looked like a Cheltenham Gold Cup winner to all of us.

The paddock was nothing like as packed as Cheltenham and we had enough space to be able to eye up the other runners. It was hard to pick out exactly who were the big dangers. The Whitbread is often won by a horse at the bottom of the weights (as Harwell Lad had been the year before) and despite Dawn running off his pre-Cheltenham handicap mark he was still the second highest in the weights with eleven stone eight pounds. Only Go Ballistic carried more weight than Dawn. At the bottom of the handicap, carrying ten stone, came the second favourite Caribou Gold. He had been second in the amateurs' handicap at Cheltenham and was an out-and-out stayer. Other horses prominent in the betting were David Nicholson's runner Call It A Day, who carried ten stone ten pounds, and Martin Pipe's runner Eudipe with eleven stone. But the only real oddity in the handicap was Dawn. If he ran up to his Cheltenham form he should win easily. If he didn't, the race seemed very open indeed.

The pressures could not have been more different from Cheltenham. There, we were the ignored underdogs. No one, least of all us, expected anything of Dawn and the thrill and excitement was all because it was so totally unexpected. But at the Whitbread it was quite the reverse. Dawn was the favourite and everyone, including the fan club, thought he should win. Winning was the only thing that would meet our expectations and there was nothing he could do that would exceed them. The television cameras tracked his movements in the pre-race build-up and if all didn't go well there would be no hiding place at all.

As the runners went down to the start we all climbed up the stairs to the main stands. Unlike Cheltenham there didn't seem to be a big screen showing the TV pictures so I had to use my binoculars. My hands were shaking as usual. I desperately wanted Dawn to prove that his Cheltenham form was genuine but were we starting to get greedy? I couldn't shake the nagging worry that this time I really had used up all my luck.

The three-mile-five-furlong start is just after the Pond fence to the right of the stands. The runners jump the two fences in the finishing straight, come past the stands and then do two full circuits of the track. I was getting better at using binoculars with shaking hands and I had them firmly focused on Andrew and Dawn as the starter dropped the tape and they were off. Dawn bounded into the lead as usual and leapt the first two fences with ease. It was lovely to see him out there looking beautiful and confident, really enjoying himself. He came past the stands with the other nineteen horses strung out in a line behind him, setting a fair old pace for a long-distance chase. 'He just might do it,' was my over-eager thought as he and Andrew headed down towards the back straight. The first circuit was fairly uneventful. Andrew had Dawn jumping brilliantly and the strong pace seemed to have some of the other horses struggling. They came past the stands and headed off for the final circuit looking every inch the Gold Cup winners. Could the fairytale continue? I dared to hope. Dawn thundered down the hill and with a mile and a bit to go the race really started to hot up. Five or six horses were only a length or so behind Dawn, he hadn't got rid of all his opposition just yet. Andrew drove him into the open ditch and Dawn stood back a mile from it, soared over and gained a length in the air. Surely he would win now. Towards the three railway fences and Dawn was still in command, but his pursuers were still only a length or two behind. Dawn met the third railway fence a little too close and clouted the top. Two or three horses went past him. He wasn't in the lead and suddenly looked very tired. The field started to turn for home and head up the stiff hill towards the finish but Dawn had had enough. One after another of the runners came past him and I could see that Andrew was pulling him up. The fairy-tale had come to an end. He wasn't going to win the Whitbread after all; Arkle's record would go untouched this year.

The race was won by Call It A Day and Adrian McGuire. I tried to be sporting and watch the finish and I was genuinely pleased that Adrian had won a big race after a dismal season, but I was still in shock. Our fantasy had come to a grinding halt. We climbed down the steps to greet Andrew and Dawn as they walked back to unsaddle. As I walked beside them somebody in the crowd yelled out: 'Don't worry, Dido, he doesn't owe anybody anything!' It was a really kind thought and a nice reminder that Dawn had done more than we ever imagined in our wildest dreams. He was breathing really hard – there was no doubt he had tried his best. 'We're never running again at Sandown,' said Andy Miller with feeling as he put Dawn's sweat rug over him, and there was no disagreement from trainer, jockey or owner. Sandown just wasn't our lucky place. Dawn had run there three times and none of them had been good days. Andrew felt that the distance had proved too much for him in the soft ground. He hadn't stayed the trip and that was that.

We all retired to the bar for a drink and tried to console ourselves. In many ways it was a good thing that Dawn hadn't won. It would mean a lot less pressure on us all when he ran again at the beginning of next season. Also, he had to lose sometime didn't he? It's amazing how much self-deception is involved in racing!

As the day drew to a close we had one final thing to do – to find out how Beamish and Alison Dare had got on at Larkhill. I couldn't decide which I was more worried about, that Beamish had run very badly and was injured or that he had won brilliantly with Alison on board and therefore my partners would want to remove me from the ride. Robert called John Dufosee because Louise didn't have a mobile, while I wrestled with my conscience. It seemed very uncharitable to hope that Beamish hadn't done well, but I couldn't bear to lose another ride. Robert came back grinning: 'Beamish ran really well,' he said.

'Oh God,' I thought, 'that's it, another ride lost.'

'He was second – he went just as well as he does for you.'

So it wasn't all bad news that day, it was just that the Cool Dawn fairytale had come to an end.

Ten days later Andrew's fairytale season also came to an end. Riding another of Robert's horses, Winspit, at Folkestone, he had a dreadful fall. Winspit crashed into a fence, spun sideways and landed on his shoulder on top of Andrew. Andrew's left leg was completely shattered and he was immediately whisked off to hospital. Winspit was in a worse state and had to be put down. Andrew needed fifteen screws and two plates to reconstruct his leg. His racing fairytale had also well and truly ended. He would be lucky to be back riding by October.

At the beginning of June, I started my brilliant new job with Manpower. They wanted me to spend my first month in America getting to grips with how their operations worked before it was announced that I would be taking over the UK business. After three fantastic weeks in New York, I went with my boss to meet the Chief Executive in Manpower's head office in Milwaukee. We arrived at lunchtime and by three o'clock we had both been fired. There had been a boardroom coup and the person who had hired both of us had been kicked out and we were being kicked out too. I was out of a job.

The fairytale really had ended. Dawn had lost the Whitbread, Andrew had shattered his leg and I was out of a job. But at least no one could take the Gold Cup away from us all.

Through the summer we all tried to recover from our setbacks. Andrew's leg seemed to be healing well and it looked as if he would be riding again by the end of September. Dawn opened fêtes and horse shows and loved every second of it. He was in no doubt that he was a complete superstar. He arched his neck and pricked his ears at the merest sight of a camera or a packet of polos – even when he got caught in the middle of the wellington boot-throwing competition at the local fête. Everywhere he went there were tales of bumper gambling wins in the West Country, at least one parish church was refloored on the back of a fortunate punter's luck! Though I really did feel for the Sturminster Newton turf accountant who ran out of cash.

Epilogue

So will I ride my Gold Cup winner in a race ever again? At the end of October, a week before Dawn's first race of the 1998–99 season, it didn't occur to me that I would ride him in the near future. Andrew was back and fit and well, and though I still hoped to get the ride back once or twice before the end of Dawn's career, I also hoped that the end was still a long way away. My old mantra still held true: if Dawn kept winning I had a top-class horse, but if he didn't then I would happily get back in the saddle. But racing is never predictable. Dawn was scheduled to reappear in the Desert Orchid Chase at Wincanton but he was not the only planned Alner runner. Super Tactics was also expected to run, with two stone less wight than Dawn. With three days to go before the race, Andrew decided that he would ride Super Tactics because he felt that two stone on softish ground was too much weight for Dawn to give to his stable companion. Then, to my complete amazement, he, Robert and Sally all suggested that I should take the ride on Dawn. Once asked, I didn't take mauch persuading.

All Dawn's Dorset fan club turned out in force to watch him and me in our first race together since our last, fateful effort at Wincanton roughly a year before. Dawn's return to action was trumpeted on the front page of the *Racing Post*, and we were all dreaming of another Cool Dawn fairytale.

But it was not to be. In the paddock something upset Dawn just as Robert was legging me up into the saddle and, before I knew it, Dawn reared up – just as he had done in his very first point-to-point at Badbury Rings. As he had done then, he didn't seem to know how to rear and he fell right over backwards, hurling me, face down, on to the tarmac track that surrounded the paddock. Unlike his first point-to-point, I wasn't thrown clear. I saw half a ton of horse falling towards me, then Dawn landed on top of me, kicked me as he tried to get up and, as I lay stationary on the ground, everyone, including me, thought I must be seriously injured. But luck was with us. I was bruised but ultimately okay and still mad enough to get back up into the saddle and canter down to the start. I think, in fact, both Dawn and I were still in shock. Unfortunately, I might have only been bruised but he was more seriously injured. After leading for the first two fences, he quickly lost his enthusiasm for jumping and after one circuit I pulled him up. Andrew and Super Tactics went on to win easily, while Dawn and I limped back to the racecourse stables.

It has taken two months to work out what was troubling Dawn. When he went over backwards in the paddock at Wincanton he crushed the vertebrae in his withers and that meant he jumped and raced very badly on his only two runs thereafter. He was too brave to ever be badly lame at home, but under pressure on the racecourse the pain took its toll. The very fact that he was so brave at home made it desperately hard to work out what was wrong, but now that we have, he has had the necessary treatment and appears to be 100 per cent healthy again. With six weeks to go before Cheltenham, we are all hoping that he will be fit and ready to defend his crown.

Our old enemy – the weather – appears to be going from strength to strength this season. It has rained almost constantly since December and unless the sun starts to shine soon then the ground will be far too soft for Dawn come

Cheltenham in March. So, in many ways things are not that different from last year. Dawn is a long-odds outsider for the Gold Cup, the weather looks as if it will be against us and in his last race he was pulled up due to an injury. The only difference is that no one can take that Gold Cup away from my mantelpiece.

This year's Gold Cup isn't the only race that I'm dreaming about. Just before I was fired from Manpower I used some of the Gold Cup prize money to buy another young racehorse to ride. My one unfulfilled racing ambition is to ride around the Aintree Grand National course, and this horse, Man of Steele, will probably turn out to be no good or so good that I have to hand the ride over to Andrew again, but that is a long way away. At the moment he is just a nice five-year-old point-to-pointer who has just finished his seven days' hunting before the beginning of the point-to-point season. And that's how all *National Velvet* dreams begin . . .

Appendix

Cool Dawn's English Racing Career up to the end of the
1997–98 season

Date	Meeting	Race	Jockey	Result
1994 Point-to-point season				
January				
29	Hursley Hambledon P-to-P	Maiden Div 3	Dido	First
February				
12	South Dorset P-to-P	Restricted	Dido	Second
March				
5	Beaufort P-to-P	Restricted	Dido	First
19	New Forest Buckhounds P-to-P	Restricted	Dido	Ran out
1995 Point-to-point and hunter chase season				
January				
14	Army P-to-P	Ladies' Open	Dido	First
February				
4	New Forest P-to-P	PPOA	Dido	First

Date	Meeting	Race	Jockey	Result
February				
22	Folkestone	2 mile 5 Novice Hunter Chase	Dido	Second
March				
20	New Forest Buckhounds	Mixed Open P-to-P	Dido	First
April				
1	Ascot	3 mile Novice Hunter Chase	Dido	First
May				
13	Warwick	3 mile 2 Novice Hunter Chase	Dido	Unseated rider

1996 Hunter chase season

Date	Meeting	Race	Jockey	Result
February				
23	Kempton	3 mile Hunter Chase	Dido	First
March				
14	Cheltenham	Christies Foxhunters 3 mile 2 Hunter Chase	Dido	Second
April				
8	Fairyhouse	Irish National 3 miles 5 Handicap	Conor O'Dwyer	Third

1996–97 National Hunt Season

Date	Meeting	Race	Jockey	Result
November				
9	Sandown	3 mile Handicap	Dido	Fourth

1997–98 National Hunt Season

Date	Meeting	Race	Jockey	Result
November				
8	Wincanton	3 mile Handicap	Dido	Seventh

Date	Meeting	Race	Jockey	Result
November				
22	Ascot	3 mile Handicap	Andrew	First
December				
20	Ascot	The Betterware Cup 3 mile Handicap	Andrew	First
January				
23	Ascot	3 mile Handicap	Andrew	First
February				
15	Sandown	3 mile Handicap	Andrew	Pulled up
March				
19	Cheltenham	Gold Cup 3 mile 2	Andrew	First
April				
8	Sandown	Whitbread Gold Cup 3 mile 5 Handicap	Andrew	Pulled up